Caroline Taggart

A Midnight Treasury *of* *Frightening Words*

RIZZOLI
UNIVERSE

Contents

Introduction

From ghoulies and ghosties and long-leggety beasties
And things that go bump in the night,
Good Lord, deliver us!

So wrote an anonymous bard back in the mists of time, and his playful prayer is a handy lead-in to considering frightening words or, perhaps more accurately, the frightening concepts we have come up with words for.

There's a strange contradiction in our attitude to frightening things. On the one hand, we love them: witness the way we lap up the latest vampire offering in the movie theater or on Disney Plus. On the other ... well, we're frightened by them. Hamlet's "witching time of night" and Macbeth's "secret, black, and midnight hags" evoke real fear of what might be going on at that spine-chilling hour when graves open and the spirits of the dead emerge into the world they're supposed to have left. Yet we're not above manipulating this fear for our own ends, inventing macabre creatures like Krampus and the Bogey-man to discourage children from staying up past their bedtime or to warn them of the consequences of bad behavior.

On a more serious note, there's barely a culture in the world that doesn't have some terrifying concept of Hell, the place we go after death to be punished for our sins, or at least to purge ourselves of them. Yet those who believe in such things have multifarious ways of contacting those who have passed over to "the other side" and take great comfort from them.

The idea of "the other side" also draws us into the realms of magic and witchcraft, ways in which to conjure spirits for good or evil. Over the centuries, many people have come up with myriad ways of wishing misfortune on those who have offended them or of protecting themselves from those who might cause them harm. Church and state alike have accused almost anyone whose views differ from their own of witchcraft, found an astonishing number of them guilty, and punished them in hideous ways. But modern witchcraft has put a positive spin on what would once have been considered heresy: rather than causing evil or misfortune, today's witches celebrate nature and the passing of the seasons, in rituals that predate Christianity and still crop up at festivals such as May Day and Hallowe'en.

These are the concepts this book delves into: frightening beings, frightening places, frightening objects, and some of the many experiences, past and present, that can't be explained away by science. As for the words themselves, there are monsters from New Zealand, Patagonia, and Canada's Pacific Northwest. There are mysterious creatures whose names translate as "a woman of the fairies," "wolf charmer," and, appropriately, "Master Midnight." There are words from Old English, ancient Greek, and the Sherpa language of the Himalayas. The thrill of frightening words takes us from the seductive spiderwomen of Japanese mythology to the flying saucers that the US government investigated in the aftermath of the Second World War; from the West African wax figures with apparently supernatural powers to the Irish legend of Stingy Jack that gave rise to the carved pumpkin of Hallowe'en; from the American woman said to be able to channel the words of a long-dead English poet to the Scottish equivalent of the guillotine which can still be seen in an Edinburgh museum. From *abracadabra* to *zombie* via *eldritch*, *mandrake* and *skull and crossbones*, and with something to raise the hairs on the back of everyone's neck, this is a celebration of the esoteric, the macabre, the spooky, and the just plain weird.

Abracadabra

By Abracadabra we signify
An infinite number of things.
Tis the answer to What? and How? and Why?
And Whence? and Whither?—a word whereby
The Truth (with the comfort it brings)
Is open to all who grope in night,
Crying for Wisdom's holy light.

So begins Ambrose Bierce's lengthy poetic definition of this magic word, as given in his *Devil's Dictionary* of 1911 (he attributes the poem to one Jamrac Holobom, but that is one of numerous pseudonyms he created for himself).

Bierce goes on to say that he doesn't know if the word is a noun or a verb, but the *Oxford English Dictionary* and other recent dictionaries give it only as a noun or as an interjection. In its earliest use (1565), it seems to have been a spell or incantation to cure a fever; not much later it could designate an amulet that warded off illness. The current use—as an exclamation accompanying a magic trick or a remarkable event—emerged in the early nineteenth century and largely superseded the earlier senses.

Whatever the meaning, no one is entirely sure where the word came from: the *Oxford English Dictionary* says its etymology has been "the subject of much conjecture" and cites possible but unproven sources as diverse as Thracian, Aramaic, and Hellenistic Greek. But there is surely something appealing about the idea that a term such as "abracadabra" should have sprung fully formed out of ... who knows where?

Alchemy

A field of supposed science, widely practiced across Europe from as far back as the fourteenth century; its aims were to find a way of turning base metal into gold (known as the philosopher's stone), and to discover an elixir granting immortality and curing all diseases. The *al-* part of the word is a corruption of the Arabic for "the," also found in algebra, alcohol, and a number of other common words; the *-chemy* (as in chemistry) is suggestive of transmutation or change.

With chemistry as we know it today in its infancy, this combination of magic and scientific method—mixing metals and salts to produce a chemical reaction—was sufficiently highly regarded for the great polymaths Paracelsus (in the sixteenth century) and Isaac Newton (in the seventeenth and eighteenth) to study it and to write extensively about it. In fact, the first line of the first book of Paracelsus's *Nine Books of the Nature of Things* reads: "The generation of all natural things is twofold: Naturall, and without Art; and Artificiall, *viz.* by Alchymie." He also maintained that it was possible for people to be born "not of a Woman in a naturall way: but by the Art, and industry of a skilfull Alchymist"—some 400 years before the first successful *in vitro* fertilization.

The eighteenth-century Age of Enlightenment, with its vast increase in what we now consider true scientific knowledge, rather eclipsed alchemy, and when interest in the subject revived during the nineteenth and early twentieth centuries the concept changed radically. Much of the credit for this goes to the Swiss psychologist Carl Jung (1875–1961) whose book *Psychology and Alchemy* compared the alchemical process of turning something impure (lead) into something pure (gold) to what he called individuation or personal growth. A modern expert in the history of science, Lawrence W. Principe, of Johns Hopkins University in Baltimore, summed up the change in a 2011 article in the journal *Isis*:

> *... occultists reinterpreted alchemy as a spiritual practice, involving the self-transformation of the practitioner and only incidentally or not at all the transformation of laboratory substances.*

Angurvadel

In Icelandic mythology, this is the sword belonging to Frithiof, hero of the epic *Frithiof's Saga,* which dates from about 1300. The name has, mysteriously, been translated both as "stream of anguish" and as "brother of lightning." According to the saga, Angurvadel was forged long ago by dwarfs in some far eastern land and Frithiof's ancestors performed many heroic deeds with it. The hilt was of hammered gold and the blade covered with strange runes that only those who had forged it could understand:

> *When Frithiof drew it from the sheath, it flashed like the lightning or the streaming Northern Lights. Moreover, a magic power belonged to this wondrous heirloom: so long as peace ruled the land the runes on the blade gleamed dull and pale, but when war prevailed they burned red as the comb of a fighting cock.*

For other powerful mythological swords, see BALISARDA (page 20).

Apocalyptic

The Apocalypse, as described in the New Testament Book of Revelation, is neither more nor less than the end of the world. The word comes from post-Classical Latin and Greek and means "uncovering" or, indeed, "revelation." Spelled with a capital and used in a theological context, it refers to the Second Coming of Christ, which goes hand in hand with the Last Judgment, deciding who will be granted eternal salvation (that is, be admitted into Heaven) or condemned to Hell. According to the biblical text, the Four Horseman of the Apocalypse—representing pestilence, famine, war, and death—are released from a sealed scroll held by God and promptly set about spreading their influence around the globe.

All pretty unpleasant. And, more importantly, life-changing. If you describe something as apocalyptic, whether you mean it literally, as with a pestilence or famine, or metaphorically, as with, say, the collapse of the stock market, you're suggesting that nothing will ever be the same again.

Arcane

From the Latin for "to shut up" or "to put away," as in a chest, this means hidden, secret, with the suggestion that, even if you discovered whatever it was that had been hidden away, it would be difficult to understand. You need to be initiated into its secrets, which are often magical or suggest CLAIRVOYANT knowledge (see page 49). In the TAROT (see page 224), the cards are divided into the Major and Minor Arcana, "arcana" being the plural of the Latin noun *arcanum*, meaning a hidden thing, a deep secret. The cards of the Major Arcana in particular, with names such as The High Priestess, The Hanged Man, Wheel of Fortune, and Death, promise to reveal hidden truths to those who dare to ask.

In a non-magical context, the word "arcane" can be used more loosely. The classical pianist Emmanuel Ax (born 1949) once remarked that "We seem to have set up some very arcane rules as to when it is actually OK to applaud," while the journalist William Safire (1929–2009), always generous in passing on his experience to less battle-hardened colleagues, warned against what he called "insiderisms":

> *Fledgling columnists, eager to impress readers with their grasp of journalistic jargon, are drawn to such arcane spellings as "lede." Where they lede, do not follow.*

Athame

The medieval text known as the *Key of Solomon* is one of the most influential of its kind, giving detailed instructions about conjuring spirits in all sorts of magic, whether evil or benevolent. Among the tools it says are necessary to the successful magician (alongside a sword, a sickle, a dagger, a wand, and others) is a knife with a black handle "for making the Circle, wherewith to strike terror and fear into the Spirits." This knife should be prepared "in the day and hour of Saturn, and dipped in the blood of a black cat and in the juice of HEMLOCK" (see page 108); various characters and names should be written on it and, once all this is done, it should be wrapped in a black silk cloth.

Such a knife may be called an "athame" (pronounced as three syllables) or an *arthame* (two syllables, a borrowing from French). Both forms can be traced back to post-Classical Latin and are found in various early versions of the *Key of Solomon*, but they took on a new lease of life in the first half of the twentieth century when students of the OCCULT (see page 176) such as the Frenchman Émile-Jules Grillot de Givry (1874–1929) and Englishman Gerald Gardner (1884–1964) began writing extensively on the subject and revived interest in the tools of the magician's trade.

B

Babadook

Created by the Australian filmmaker Jennifer Kent for her 2014 psychological thriller of the same name, this is an adaptation of Baba Yaga (see page 18) and other similar names for Bogey-man (see page 31) -type monsters. In the movie, the Babadook begins life as the top-hatted central character in a child's pop-up book, but he soon escapes from its pages and causes mayhem and horror: the mother in the story has visions of herself killing the family dog, her son, and eventually herself, all under the Babadook's influence. Kent is quoted as saying that she wanted to tell a story about the darkness we feel within ourselves, the "fear of going mad," and, even more darkly, the struggle some parents have in their relationships with their children.

Baba Yaga

Many cultures have a frightening mythical creature whom parents may invoke to encourage children to behave, and Baba Yaga fulfils this role in Russia and many parts of Eastern Europe. The name varies slightly from language to language, but the character remains largely the same. *Baba* means "old woman" or "grandmother" in various Slavic tongues and, while the derivation of *yaga* is less clear, it may mean something along the lines of evil, furious, or abusive. Baba Yaga's particular way of dealing with naughty children is to fry them and eat them; she is sometimes depicted flying around in a mortar, wielding a pestle (the club-like implement you use for crushing garlic); her home is a hut in the forest built on chickens' legs.

Baba Yaga doesn't always have everything her own way. In one story, her house is surrounded by twelve poles. On eleven of these is stuck a human head, while the twelfth is alarmingly—invitingly?—unoccupied. Whatever plans Baba Yaga may have had for this last pole, it remains vacant, as she is outsmarted by the hero of the story and drowns. In another variant, she is again outwitted, this time by a little girl—apparently her niece—whom she wants to eat for breakfast; the moral here is that if she had been kinder to her maidservant and her cat, they would not have taken the niece's side against her. Perhaps this, too, is intended to be a lesson to naughty children: be kind to animals, and to those less well off than yourself.

See also Bogey-man (page 31).

Baleful

"Bale" is an archaic word meaning evil, injury, or pain. To be baleful, then, is to be full of bale, harmful, threatening, destructive, even deadly. John Milton, in the opening section of his epic *Paradise Lost* (1667), describes Satan, the fallen angel cast out from Heaven, now lying vanquished in the "fiery gulf" that is Hell:

> *... now the thought*
> *Both of lost happiness and lasting pain*
> *Torments him: round he throws his baleful eyes,*
> *That witnessed huge affliction and dismay,*
> *Mixed with obdurate pride and steadfast hate.*

See also SATANIC (page 197).

Balisarda

Many legends contain stories of heroes with magical swords—King Arthur's Excalibur is probably the most famous one; there's also Arondight, "the sword of truth," which belonged to Sir Lancelot, the finest swordsman in Arthurian legend. It glowed with unearthly brilliance when wielded by its rightful owner and could withstand any attack without being damaged. However, its power depended on Lancelot remaining pure and chivalrous, and was much diminished when he broke his vows of chastity and loyalty by having an affair with King Arthur's wife Guinevere.

But Balisarda is a sword that deserves particular mention. It belonged to the Saracen Ruggiero in *Orlando Furioso* ("The Frenzy of Orlando"), a highly influential Italian epic poem of the sixteenth century, written by Ludovico Ariosto. The sword is said to have been made by a sorceress and to be capable of slicing through enchanted objects. At one point in the narrative we are told that, although Ruggiero's adversary was "encased in steel plate and iron mail," he seemed unprotected against Balisarda; and at another that "where Balisarda bites no spells avail."

The name seems to have been adapted from *baselard*, an old word for a type of long dagger.

See also Angurvadel (page 11).

Banshee

Meaning literally "a woman of the fairies or elves," in Irish folklore this an ominous female spirit who wails to announce an impending death. In casual use, "howling like a banshee" can describe anyone who is making a lot of unpleasant noise.

Not everyone has the honor of having their passing heralded by a banshee, however. The Scottish novelist Sir Walter Scott, in his *Letters on Demonology and Witchcraft* (1829), records that he has been told that the privilege is "only allowed to families of the pure Milesian stock"—that is, families descended from a tribe of people (the sons of Mil) who had settled in Ireland before the ninth century. It is "never ascribed to any descendant of the proudest Norman or boldest Saxon" who invaded Ireland in the twelfth century, much less to "adventurers of later date who have obtained settlements in the Green Isle."

So, whereas in some cultures the way you speak and whether or not your family owns an ancestral home are signs of distinction, in Ireland it's the howl of the banshee that testifies to your pedigree.

Basilisk

Also known as the *cockatrice*, this animal, according to Thomas Bulfinch, a nineteenth-century American authority on fables, was "called the king of the serpents" and "supposed to be produced from the egg of a cock, hatched under toads or serpents." Crowned with a crest or comb (hence the alternative name), the basilisk could kill anyone it looked upon through the mere power of its gaze. Shakespeare was obviously familiar with this idea: in his *King Richard III* (ca. 1592), the villainous Richard is paying court to Lady Anne, who makes no bones about how much she hates him:

> *Anne: Out of my sight! Thou dost infect mine eyes.*
> *Richard: Thine eyes, sweet lady, have infected mine.*
> *Anne: Would they were basilisks, to strike thee dead!*

Whoever first called this creature a basilisk must have had a certain amount of respect for it, or at least admiration for its appearance: as with the given name Basil, the derivation of the word can be traced back to the Greek for king.

Beelzebub

One of many names for the Devil, this derives from the Hebrew for "lord of the flies"; it is also connected with *Baal,* which means simply "lord" but was the name of the principal god of the Phoenicians and Canaanites. In Old Testament lore *Baal* came to mean any false god—that is, not the "true" god worshipped by the Jews.

Beelzebub was popular with seventeenth-century writers. In John Bunyan's *The Pilgrim's Progress* (1678) he is designated simply as "the enemy of our Lord," while in the opening section of Milton's *Paradise Lost* (1667), when the poet is considering how Adam and Eve came to be cast out of the Garden of Eden, we find this description of the fall of the "infernal Serpent" who was responsible for leading them into temptation:

There the companions of his fall, o'erwhelmed
With floods and whirlwinds of tempestuous fire,
He soon discerns; and, weltering by his side,
One next himself in power, and next in crime,
Long after known in Palestine, and named
Beelzebub.

Second only to the Serpent in terms of crime: that puts Beelzebub high up on anybody's list of evil beings.

Behemoth

In the Old Testament Book of Job, God appears to Job and, blasphemous though it may sound, basically boasts about all the things He has created. One of them is Behemoth, a monster that many have since assumed is the same as a hippopotamus:

> *Look at Behemoth, which I made along with you and which feeds on grass like an ox. What strength it has in its loins, what power in the muscles of its belly! Its tail sways like a cedar; the sinews of its thighs are close-knit. Its bones are tubes of bronze, its limbs like rods of iron.*

The word may come from the Hebrew for beast, or from the Egyptian for water-ox (which would strengthen the connection to hippopotamus, meaning literally "river horse"). Today a behemoth is any large, strong, and unwieldy thing, less complicated than a LEVIATHAN (see page 136) but almost as unstoppable as a JUGGERNAUT (see page 128).

Belladonna

Also known as deadly nightshade, belladonna is a poisonous plant related both to the potato and to tobacco. Its name comes from the Italian for "beautiful lady," because women used to use it as a cosmetic—Cleopatra is said to have used a related plant, Egyptian HENBANE (see page 109), to dilate her pupils and increase her sex appeal.

These women would have been ill advised to eat the plant's berries, though. The sixteenth-century herbalist John Gerard records that "this kind of nightshade causes sleep, troubles the mind, brings madness if a few of the berries be inwardly taken, but if more be given they also kill and bring present death." He goes on to counsel: "Banish therefore these pernicious plants out of your gardens."

Not everyone took his advice. Belladonna, alongside opium poppies and other poisonous plants such as HEMLOCK (see page 108) and MONKSHOOD (see page 159), was an ingredient in the so-called "flying ointment" of European folklore that witches rubbed into their skins to enable them to fly to meet others of their kind, though both belladonna and opium have properties that have led some to suggest that they induced not so much literal flying as a hallucinogenic trip. In ancient times belladonna had been associated with the wine god Dionysus and could be mixed into a drink that either sent worshippers into a trance or released their inhibitions sufficiently for them to enjoy a drunken frenzy.

In the nineteenth century the key ingredient atropine was isolated and belladonna began to be utilized in various medicines; it was sufficiently easy to come by that Sherlock Holmes could use it—in "The Adventure of the Dying Detective" (1913)—to persuade people that he was dying. When at the end of the story this is revealed to have been a plot, and Watson asks him to explain his appearance, his "ghastly face," Holmes replies:

> *Three days of absolute fast does not improve one's beauty, Watson. For the rest, there is nothing which a sponge may not cure. With vaseline upon one's forehead, belladonna in one's eyes, rouge over the cheek-bones, and crusts of beeswax round one's lips, a very satisfying effect can be produced. Malingering is a subject upon which I have sometimes thought of writing a monograph.*

Belomancy

A form of divination using arrows. A nineteenth-century *History of Magic* describes it as an ancient practice, and there are two incidences of it in the Old Testament. The first occurs in the Second Book of Kings, when the prophet Elisha is on his deathbed; he instructs Joash, King of Judah, to fire arrows from an east-facing window and prophesies that this is "the arrow of the Lord's deliverance, and the arrow of deliverance from Syria." In the Book of Ezekiel, the King of Babylon "stands at the parting of the ways" and uses arrows to help him decide which route to take.

The word comes, via Latin, from the Greek for arrows or darts, plus the suffix *-mancy* used in a variety of words to do with divination: see NECROMANCY (page 167).

Beltane

See WALPURGISNACHT (page 248).

Bodeful

A rare word, but one that it would be a shame to lose, as it is redolent of darkness ahead, of mysterious and unnerving threat. The obsolete noun "bode" meant a premonition or omen; as a verb, the word is still in use in expressions such as "that bodes ill," meaning it's a bad sign, it will end badly. Bodeful, then, means full of bode, ominous. The American critic James Russell Lowell, writing in 1870 about Lady Macbeth's reference to the raven, describes her as hearing "the voice of the bodeful bird," predicting disaster. The more commonly used "foreboding"—a feeling that some unknown disaster is about to strike—comes from the same Old English source.

Body-snatcher

The meaning may seem obvious, but the concept is a specific one: according to James Hardy Vaux's 1812 *New and Comprehensive Vocabulary of the Flash Language* (where "flash" means thieves' slang), it denotes "a stealer of dead bodies from churchyards; which are sold to the surgeons and students in anatomy." Before the Anatomy Act of 1832, it was illegal in the United Kingdom to dissect any corpse except that of an executed criminal. As interest in the study of anatomy grew, so did the demand for bodies, and with it the opportunity for graverobbers to make money from fulfilling this demand.

Jerry Cruncher, a character in Dickens's *A Tale of Two Cities* (published in 1859, but set around the time of the French Revolution of sixty years earlier, when body-snatching would have been thriving) practices this profession, although Dickens doesn't use the term, preferring to describe him as an "honest tradesman" or, to use another euphemism current at the time, a "resurrection man."

Bogey-man

Sometimes spelled boogey-man, bogy-man or just bogey/boogey/bogy, this is a name of unknown origin that may be related to "bug" in the sense of terror, as in "bugbear," meaning an object of needless dread. The Bogey-man is a character in English-speaking countries whose role is largely to scare naughty children into going to bed on time. According to some traditions he's a shadowy, shapeless figure who hides in dark places and can be frightened away by bright light.

Nor is his influence confined to children: William Makepeace Thackeray, in an 1853 critique of William Hogarth's satirical series of paintings *Marriage à la Mode*, observes that the people in it are all "naughty"—a stronger word in Thackeray's day than it is now—"and Bogie carries them all off." So the Bogey-man is not just a threat about what will happen if you stay up past your bedtime, it's also a warning about what befalls if (to quote Thackeray again) you marry a man for his rank or a woman for her money.

Many other cultures have equivalent terrifying creatures that harassed parents can call on. In Brazil, wakeful children may be threatened with the *Cuca* or Crocodile Lady, while the Algerian *H'awouahoua* is a particularly gruesome character with eyes that are globules of flaming spit and garments made from the clothes of children he has eaten. See also Baba Yaga (page 18), Butzemann (page 37), and Krampus (page 133), to name but three more.

Boggard

Also spelled boggart, this is a word of uncertain derivation from the North of England, where it means a specter or Bogey-man (see page 31) supposed to haunt a gloomy place. In Georgette Heyer's 1959 novel *The Unknown Ajax,* set in the early nineteenth century, a character from Yorkshire visiting the marshy areas of Kent and Sussex for the first time finds the landscape eerie; he wonders if people meet "flay-boggards" if they go out at night and, when asked to translate, explains that he means hobgoblins (see page 112). The "flay" part is another northern dialect word, meaning a fright.

Bogle

The Scots term for a frightening GHOST (see page 84) or PHANTOM (see page 184). Of uncertain origin but possibly connected with a Welsh word for fear, it emerged in Scotland in the sixteenth century and was adopted into English in the nineteenth, where boggle (as in "the mind boggles") became a more common spelling. The poet Robert Southey wrote, in a letter of 1832, that:

> *Boggles and Barquests are the only supernatural beings we hear of in these parts [the English Lake District]; to what class they belong I cannot tell you; but the Barquest, which I believe, generally appears in the shape of some quadruped, may possibly in its origin have simply been a mountain spirit.*

Other sources tell us that barquest (or barguest or barghest) appeared in much of northern England in its day, generally taking the form of a large and threatening black dog, with eyes the size of saucers. It didn't haunt particular spots but roamed over wide areas, often including graveyards; according to one report it was fatal to catch its eye. Southey's letter, however, adds the comforting rider:

> *Large towns and large manufactories in the country destroy all superstitions of this kind.*

Bokkenrijder

The Dutch equivalent of the BOGEY-MAN (see page 31), this translates literally as "buck rider" or "goat rider." The *bokkenrijder* does indeed ride a flying goat and terrorizes local farming communities, though the story goes that this legend was deliberately created by bands of eighteenth-century thieves, presumably to throw the blame for their misdeeds on something less tangible than themselves.

Boo

The simplest and most basic of scary words, "boo" first appeared in the early seventeenth century in the expression "wouldn't say boo (or sometimes *bo* or *boh*) to a goose," used to describe someone very timid who couldn't stand up for themselves. Boo soon became an interjection on its own, intended to scare people by taking them by surprise. By the late eighteenth century, it could be a way of expressing disapproval or disbelief—a footnote in Maria Edgeworth's 1800 novel *Castle Rackrent* tells its readers that it is equivalent to "pshaw" or "nonsense"—and another hundred years later it had also developed into something you might shout during a bad play or a soccer match where you disagreed with the referee.

So where did it come from? Well, the *Oxford English Dictionary* describes it as "an imitative or expressive formation": it says the same about "boh" and "pooh." In phonetics, the "B" sound is what's called a voiced bilabial plosive, which means it uses both lips, a vibration of the vocal cords, and closure and reopening of the vocal tract to give a sort of popping sound. In lay terms, words beginning with B are quite satisfying to shout. And the long vowel of boo can be turned into the haunting—or disapproving—boooooo in a way that the more abrupt boh simply can't.

Booooo

Brimstone

From the Old English for "burning stone," this used to be the common name for sulfur but is now chiefly used with reference to the fact that it burns—often in the expression "fire and brimstone." The Old Testament Book of Genesis tells us that God rained brimstone and fire down on the sinful cities of Sodom and Gomorrah in order to destroy them; and when, toward the end of the New Testament Book of Revelation, the final battle between good and evil comes, a false prophet is "cast alive into a lake of fire burning with brimstone."

On a more temporal level, a medicinal mixture of brimstone and treacle or molasses was a recognized cure-all in Victorian times, notably used, in Dickens's *Nicholas Nickleby* (1839), by the sadistic schoolmaster Mr Squeers who also features under SINISTER (see page 208). As Mrs Squeers explains to Nicholas, newly arrived to teach at the school:

> *"They have the brimstone and treacle, partly because if they hadn't something or other in the way of medicine they'd be always ailing and giving a world of trouble, and partly because it spoils their appetites and comes cheaper than breakfast and dinner. So, it does them good and us good at the same time, and that's fair enough I'm sure."*

Brimstone and treacle attained still more disquieting associations when the playwright Dennis Potter used it as the title of a 1976 television play (made into a 1982 movie starring Sting). In Potter's work, a middle-aged couple find that the young man who has moved into their North London home on the pretext of a previous relationship with their vulnerable daughter has demonic powers.

In other words, from Biblical times to suburban London in the twentieth century and in many and various ways, brimstone has been able to wreak havoc pretty much everywhere.

Butzemann

Another Bogey-man (see page 31), this time a German one. He features in a harmless children's song about a jolly fellow who dances around the house, shaking himself and throwing his sack over his shoulder, but his origins are more sinister. He is variously described as a poltergeist (see page 186) with rattling bones and a scythe; a faceless goblin swathed in a cloak who hides in dark corners or cupboards or under the bed; and a demon or spirit who brings apples to well-behaved children but carries the naughty ones away in his sack.

German mythology is full of creatures like this—see Krampus (page 133) for another. There is also the *Nachtkrapp* or the Night Raven who will sneak into children's rooms at night to steal them from their beds and eat any that set eyes on him. There's a very strong theme of "Go to sleep or else" running through all these tales.

The Pennsylvania Dutch community in the USA have adopted the Butzemann in a more benevolent guise: to them, he has become the magical scarecrow who protects crops throughout the growing season before being burned (as an effigy) on Hallowe'en (see page 102).

Cadaverous

The word "cadaver" is a direct borrowing from Latin and means a human corpse, often one that is used for dissection. So, a cadaver is, by definition, dead. If you describe someone as "cadaverous," however, they are likely to be alive, but unhealthy looking and painfully thin. *The Cambridge English Dictionary* gives this fine example of how the adjective is used:

> *They appear as cadaverous humanoid creatures that attack at close range with their claws and from a distance by vomiting projectiles of green goo.*

Sadly, it doesn't tell us who "they" are, but it's safe to assume we should avoid them if we can.

For more about the use of cadavers in the study of anatomy, and the illicit way they were acquired, see BODY-SNATCHER (page 30). If you prefer to keep on the right side of the law, Mary Roach's 2003 book *Stiff: the Curious Lives of Human Cadavers* considers many legal ways in which cadavers have been used over the years: they helped to test France's first guillotine, were used by Russian embalmers in the early twentieth century, and played a key role in persuading the US Congress to make it mandatory to wear seat belts. Roach also gives a notably matter-of-fact definition of the word: "You are a person and then you cease to be a person, and a cadaver takes your place."

Calaca

A colloquial word for skull or skeleton in Mexican Spanish, used as part of the Day of the Dead festivities there.

The Day of the Dead is the equivalent of All Souls' Day (see HALLOWE'EN, page 102), and is a big festival in Latin America, spilling over onto various days before and after. The *calaca* can take the form of a doll with a skull for a face, either life-size or table-top, used as a decoration; it is often depicted wearing a big hat, adorned with marigolds, whose powerful scent and bright orange color are said to guide the dead back into the land of the living. People taking part in the festivities may dress as *calacas*, and highly decorated skulls made out of sugar (*calaveras de azúcar* or "sugar skulls") also form a key part of the celebrations.

The whole idea—based on an old Aztec belief—is that the dead would prefer to be celebrated than mourned, so the day is marked by singing, dancing, and revelry. The underlying theme of the 2017 Pixar movie *Coco*, set at the time of the Day of the Dead, is that the deceased continue to have some form of life as long as their loved ones remember them. And if they choose to wear big hats with marigolds on them, so much the better.

Carrion flower

You might not expect there to be many plants that smelled of rotting flesh, but in fact they are found on at least three continents (Asia, Africa, and North America) and can belong to one of at least five genera—*Amorphophallus, Rafflesia, Stapelia, Smilax,* and *Bulbophyllum.* This means that they can be anything from an orchid to a cactus-like succulent. Also nicknamed stinking flower or corpse flower, they produce the smell to attract pollinators and other creatures that are enticed by actual rotting flesh. The American philosopher Henry David Thoreau came across the *Smilax* version and recorded in his 1852 journal that it was:

> *... a rank green vine ... It smells exactly like a dead rat in the wall,—*
> *& apparently attracts flies like carrion.*

Mycologists might like to know that the stinkhorn fungus of the widespread and graphically named Phallaceae family operates according to the same pungent principle.

Catacomb

In the first centuries of the Christian era, when the religion was illegal and its practitioners persecuted, they were in dire need of cheap mass graves. The original catacombs—on the Appian Way just outside Rome—have miles of tunnels with vaults and niches leading off them, serving as tombs for those early Christians. The word probably derives from the name of the place and has come to be applied to any similar underground burial site. There are impressive catacombs in Paris, covering about 800 hectares. These date only from the eighteenth century and are said to house the remains of six million people, many of whom were transferred there under cover of darkness from the city's overflowing cemeteries. *The Penny Cyclopedia*, published in the 1830s and '40s by the London-based Society for the Diffusion of Useful Knowledge, tells us—not mincing its words—that, by a recent decree of the French government:

> ... *all the churchyards were emptied of their contents, and the skulls and bones sent to the spacious subterranean quarries, where they are now arranged in a manner that is grotesquely horrible.*

Even so, tourists today flock to participate in guided tours, as they do to the Italian original.

Cauldron

The dictionary definition of cauldron doesn't lead you to believe it has any connection with witchery: from the Latin for hot, it's simply a large pot used for boiling, particularly one with handles. But the association with magic powers goes back hundreds of years. In the *Mabinogion*—the earliest known collection of Welsh prose, dating from the twelfth or thirteenth century—there is mention of a cauldron with the ability to bring a slain warrior back to life, to be "as well as ever he was at the best," except that he will not regain the power of speech. The same work also features a "cauldron of Inspiration and Science," in which a selection of charm-bearing plants must be boiled for a year and a day until they produce three blessed drops of a liquid that will enable whoever drinks them to see into the future.

But we can probably blame Shakespeare for enduringly linking the cauldron to witches. Act IV, Scene i of *Macbeth* (1606) is set in "A dark Cave. In the middle, a Cauldron Boiling," and it's in this scene that the three witches utter the famous words:

> *Double, double, toil and trouble;*
> *Fire, burn; and cauldron, bubble.*

At the time, a cauldron would have been the obvious container for anyone to use for boiling anything, for good or evil—on the face of it, these words are no more sinister than an impatient person in a modern kitchen urging a kettle to boil (but for more about what the witches are up to, see HAG, page 101). However, given that no one uses a cauldron any more, unless they are cooking over an open fire, it's no surprise that Shakespeare's memorable words should have sealed this inoffensive utensil's fate as a witch's vessel of choice.

Changeling

Before the action of Shakespeare's *A Midsummer Night's Dream* begins, Oberon and Titania, king and queen of the fairies, have fallen out. At an early stage in the play, Puck, servant to Oberon, warns one of Titania's followers not to let the queen come near her husband, who is angry:

> ... *Because that she, as her attendant, hath*
> *A lovely boy, stol'n from an Indian king;*
> *She never had so sweet a changeling.*
> *And jealous Oberon would have the child*
> *Knight of his train.*

Titania refuses to part with the boy, and her intransigence sparks the various misunderstandings and mistaken identities of the plot.

In this context, a changeling is clearly a child stolen from this world and taken to the fairy kingdom. More usually it is the other way round: a child said to have been left in exchange for one the fairies have taken away. The *-ling* part of the word indicates "belonging to a group," often with a suggestion of contempt: Martians in early science-fiction comics, for example, used to refer to earthlings, and a person who works for someone else and isn't highly regarded may be an underling. Thus, in day-to-day parlance, a changeling can be a cheap replacement for something superior, or a child who for some reason doesn't resemble their parents. An artist in a family of accountants—or indeed an accountant in a family of artists—could be described, one hopes jokingly, as a changeling.

The original, fairy-linked concept is widespread in European folklore, with some cultures suggesting that trolls do the swap in order to procure a—presumably superior—human upbringing for their own children. There are various means of protecting your babies against being stolen. Not washing their nappies after sunset is one; placing an iron tool such as a pair of scissors on top of the cradle (because in Nordic tradition supernatural beings are afraid of iron) is another. If these measures fail and the baby is abducted, taking the changeling to Cornwall and passing it through the hole in one of the Mên-an-Tol stones may help reverse the spell, thanks to the magical powers of the stone's guardian spirits.

Chimera

In Greek mythology, the Chimera or Chimaera was a fire-breathing monster with the head of a lion, the body of a goat, and the tail of a serpent or dragon. Thomas Bulfinch tells us that the monster was causing "great havoc" in the kingdom of Lycia (in modern Turkey), so that the Lycian king was anxious to find a warrior to kill it. Enter the young hero Bellerophon, who, with the goddess Minerva on his side and the winged horse Pegasus to help him, won an easy victory over the Chimera.

Appropriately enough given the makeup of the beast, the word "chimera" comes from various sources, including Middle English, Greek, Latin, and French, and today tends to mean something less fearsome than the original: not so much a monster as an unrealistic idea or pipe dream. As early as 1726, the Irish satirist Jonathan Swift was writing sardonically in *Gulliver's Travels* of a people who:

> *... were proposing schemes for persuading monarchs to choose favourites upon the score of their wisdom, capacity, and virtue; of teaching ministers to consult the public good; of rewarding merit, great abilities, eminent services ... of choosing for employments persons qualified to exercise them, with many other wild, impossible chimeras, that never entered before into the heart of man to conceive.*

In other words, none of these things is ever going to happen.

Choreomania

From the Greek for dance and the Latin for madness, choreomania means precisely what that etymology suggests: a dancing madness, also known as *chorea* or St Vitus's dance. In much of Europe from the fourteenth to the seventeenth centuries there seems to have been an epidemic of this "madness," which took the form of seizures, convulsions, and dancing. Victims, who could be either adults or children, sometimes literally danced themselves to death. No one is certain what caused these attacks—the best guess by scholars is that it was some kind of mass hysteria, but it remains a medical mystery. At the time, however, the possibility that sufferers were possessed by demons could not be ignored and many EXORCISMS (see page 71) were performed. Prayers were also offered to two saints who some believed had sent the affliction: one was St John the Baptist, the cousin of Christ; the other St Vitus, a Sicilian martyr of the third and fourth centuries, whose feast day was traditionally celebrated with dancing.

Chronophage

On the outside wall of the library of Corpus Christi College, Cambridge, is displayed a clock topped by a huge grasshopper that is part of the mechanism: according to its creator, the inventor and horologist John C. Taylor, the whole is built of materials (including gold) chosen for their longevity. It was Taylor who, for the unveiling in 2008, coined the name Chronophage, derived from Greek words that translate as "time eater"; as he puts it, "The creatures that stalk the top of the clocks will continue to eat time for hundreds of years to come." Surely a concept to rival J.K. Rowling's Death Eaters for unexpressed but spine-tingling menace.

Chupacabra

The 2023 movie *Chupa* tells of a scientist on a quest to find a chupacabra in Mexico because of its supposed medicinal powers, and of the local youngsters determined to protect the chupacabra cub they have befriended. They thus embark, the publicity says, on "the adventure of a lifetime."

This movie, and others featuring similar creatures, have done much to heighten awareness of the chupacabra. Its name derived from Spanish words meaning "goat-sucker," it is a VAMPIRE-like creature (see page 243) of Latin-American, and particularly Puerto Rican, myth that feeds not necessarily on goats but on any domestic animals. It then leaves their carcasses uneaten but drained of blood.

Supposed eye-witness reports describe an animal that resembles either a fierce, hairless dog or a reptilian kangaroo with large, red eyes but, strangely enough, scientific evidence to back up these reports seems to be lacking.

Clairvoyant

From the French for "seeing clearly," this means apparently being able to see beyond the normal range of perception: having a "sixth sense," foretelling the future, communicating with the dead, and so on. The word came into English in the middle of the nineteenth century, when interest in the supposed science of the OCCULT (see page 176) was very much in vogue.

Views on the validity of clairvoyancy vary. The spiritualist Charles Webster Leadbeater (1854–1934) believed:

> *The clairvoyant is simply a man who develops within himself the power to respond to another octave out of the stupendous gamut of possible vibrations, and so enables himself to see more of the world around him than those of more limited perception.*

Ambrose Bierce, author of the 1911 *Devil's Dictionary*, was more cynical. He defined a clairvoyant as:

> *A person, commonly a woman, who has the power of seeing that which is invisible to her patron—namely, that he is a blockhead.*

A clear case of everyone being entitled to their own opinion.

Cromlech

With a name derived from the Welsh for a flat stone that is bent or arched, a cromlech consists of a large, flat stone lying on top of several standing ones, forming a burial chamber. Similar prehistoric structures are found in Brittany, where they are known as dolmen (table stones). One of the most striking examples in Britain is at Bodowyr on the island of Anglesey in Wales, where a large, mushroom-shaped capstone sits atop three supporting stones, each about 3ft (1m) high; a similar stone lying nearby suggests that there were once four supports but that one fell over sometime in the last 4,000–14,000 years. William Camden, the antiquarian who traveled around Britain in the sixteenth century and produced *Britannia*, the first topographical survey of the country, described the top stone as "somewhat gibbous or convex," but admired it as the most elegant of its kind he had seen: whereas others were "altogether rude and unpolish'd," at Bodowyr the stones were "neatly wrought, considering the natural roughness of the stone."

It was probably a communal grave, but it has never been excavated, so sadly we have no details of who might be buried there or why.

Crone

See HAG (page 101).

Cunning

The most common modern sense of this word—sly, devious, clever in getting one's own way—dates back to Shakespeare's time and beyond: there's mention of a "cunning fiend" in *Henry V* (c. 1599) and a "cunning thief" in *Cymbeline* (c. 1611). But the idea of a cunning man or cunning woman as someone possessing special, possibly magical, knowledge or skill, a fortune teller, witch (see WITCHCRAFT page 256), or WIZARD (see page 259), is older than that. The French romance of *William of Palerne*, sometimes translated as *William and the Werewolf* and written perhaps as early as the twelfth century, contains a character described as "full cunning and crafty," able to perceive many things through "charms and enchantments"; she's certainly capable of sending William to sleep and making him experience a dream of her choosing.

The idea of a cunning person persisted until at least 1807, when the future Poet Laureate Robert Southey produced a collection of letters which were supposedly written by a Spaniard making observations on English customs. He remarks that a person who has been robbed doesn't consult the parish constable, but instead:

> *... repairs to a witch or wizard to recover the loss, or learn who the criminal is, by means of a familiar spirit! A Cunning-Man, or a Cunning-Woman, as they are termed, is to be found near every town, and though the laws are occasionally put in force against them, still it is a gainful trade.*

Damoclean

Pertaining to Damocles, particularly in the expression "the sword of Damocles," referring to a man who, in the fourth century BCE, was a courtier to Dionysus I, ruler of Syracuse in Sicily. The story goes that Damocles irritated his master by talking sycophantically about how glorious it must be to be wealthy and powerful.

According to the Roman writer Cicero, the principal source of this cautionary tale, Dionysus suggested that Damocles might like to try this sort of life for himself. So, he invited his courtier to a banquet, ordered him to be laid out on a bed of gold, waited on by handsome young men, and fed "the most exquisite meats." Then, just as Damocles was thinking how happy he was, Dionysus "ordered a bright sword to be let down from the ceiling, suspended by a single horse-hair." The moment Damocles noticed this, he could no longer enjoy the luxurious surroundings, the exquisite food, or the handsome waiters—and had to admit that Dionysus had proved his point: that no one could be happy if he faced the constant threat of losing everything, as anyone in a position of power did.

"The sword of Damocles" has thus come to mean any impending disaster, and the adjective Damoclean or Damoclesian describes a situation where the worst seems likely to happen. The French philosopher Voltaire (1694–1778), living at a time when revolution was just around the corner, took an understandably gloomy view: "Life resembles the banquet of Damocles," he is often quoted as saying; "the sword is ever suspended."

Danse macabre

"Macabre dance" or "dance of death," a dance in which one or more skeletal figures, the personification of Death, lead people dancing toward the grave—the point being to show that everyone, from monarchs to paupers, is equal when death comes for them. It was a popular subject for artists for many centuries, the earliest known example being a mural in Paris's Holy Innocents cemetery dating from about 1425. Hans Holbein, best known for the paintings he did at the court of Henry VIII about a hundred years later, produced a series of woodcuts on this theme, and in 1875 the French composer Camille Saint-Saëns produced a "symphonic poem" for orchestra in which Death, emerging from the grave and playing his fiddle to lead the dance, is represented by a haunting solo violin.

It wasn't until the nineteenth century that the word "macabre" came to be used separately from the concept of the dance of death. In 1889, the literary *Athenaeum* magazine, reviewing a collection of verse by the French poet Jean Lahor (a pen name of the physician Henri Cazalis), observed:

> *One Dance of Death circles uninterruptedly from end to end ... The book is* macabre, *but unaffectedly* macabre, *without romantic pose or neurotic contortion. It is the natural effect of the dire realities of death and corruption as witnessed in hospital and dissecting-room by a medical student who is not as other medical students ...*

It's worth noting that the *Athenaeum* puts the word in italics, acknowledging that it was a borrowing from French, a language as yet unfamiliar to the average English reader.

Darkling

A versatile word, this can be a noun meaning a period of dark or when darkness falls, a verb meaning to get dark and/or gloomy, or an adjective or adverb meaning either literally dark or figuratively hidden, obscure, or mysterious. In Shakespeare's *A Midsummer Night's Dream* (c. 1595), Helena, unrequitedly in love with Demetrius, has pursued him into the forest; when he tries to get rid of her, she protests, "O, wilt thou darkling leave me? do not so." Not only is it getting dark, but—as the audience knows, even if Helena doesn't—there are fairies about and they could make mischief.

Dead man's fingers

Various plants are given this common name—there's mention of it in *Hamlet* (c. 1599), when Queen Gertrude describes the brook where Ophelia has drowned: she's probably referring to a type of orchid, also known as "long purple." But the appellation of dead man's fingers is more suited to the fungus *Xylaria polymorpha,* which grows in clusters of warty-looking digits that, according to the Woodland Trust, look "as if someone buried beneath the woodland floor is trying to make a last-ditch attempt to escape."

Alternatively, dead man's fingers can refer to the gills of a lobster or crab, which tradition has it will kill you if you eat them. (Not true, but they are definitely unpleasant.) James Beresford's *Miseries of Human Life* (1806), which includes a vast array of torments, from paper cuts to cracking a hard nut with your teeth, mentions that, when eating lobster, the trick is to avoid "getting *the Lady*, or half a dozen stripes of the dead man's fingers, into your mouth before you are aware."

Demonology

The word "demon," meaning a devil or any malevolent being, has been in use in English for over a thousand years, and has spawned many more recent terms to do with the dark arts.

From the Greek meaning "work," the suffix *-urgy* indicates an action or technology connected to the first part of the word: *metallurgy*, the study of metals, for example. Demonurgy is therefore a form of sorcery that involves demons. Demonism means a belief in them; demonography writing about them; demonolatry the worship of them. *Three Books of Demonolatry* was the title of an influential 1595 work about demons and witches, recounting many hundreds of trials (and executions) for WITCHCRAFT (see page 256) that had taken place in the Duchy of Lorraine over the preceding fifteen years. Perhaps even more influential was *Daemonologie,* published two years later: it contained an analysis of the different types of demons and of magic; the assertion that witchcraft was widely practiced in Britain by people under the influence of Satan; and an insistence that they should be tracked down and severely punished. Much of the book's importance lay in the fact that it was written by King James VI of Scotland, who would within a few years also become James I of England.

The title of James's book is the first recorded use of the word demonology (in any of its spellings), but it quickly passed into the language and spread to cover a wide range of studies and beliefs about the demonic world. By the nineteenth century, its meaning had expanded still further, to include a catalogue, real or hypothetical, of one's ideological enemies, or of beliefs of which one didn't approve: the nineteenth-century historian William Lecky, for example, observed that "In the demonology of [Karl] Marx the capitalist is the central figure." There's no suggestion that he was accusing the author of *Das Kapital* of SATANIC practices (see page 197), but Marx's dislike of capitalism is made clear.

Diabolism

From the Greek for "devil," this is worship of the Devil and any practices or rites connected with that worship. The word appeared in English in the seventeenth century, when concern about WITCHCRAFT (see page 256) and Devil worship was in the forefront of many minds, and soon developed the wider sense in which the adjective "diabolical" is used today: extremely cruel or wicked, or just outrageous, as in the expression "a diabolical liberty." Perhaps typically of British writers, early uses in this sense often refer to the weather: Walter Scott wrote in a 1796 letter of his disappointment at not being able to entertain some visitors as he would have wished: "The day being diabolical I had it not in my power to shew them the beauties of this place."

Djinn

In Islamic and pre-Islamic culture, this is a supernatural being capable of assuming human or animal form and influencing the lives of mortals. According to the orientalist Edward William Lane (1801–1876), djinns (or jinns or jinnees) were created "from a smokeless fire ... some thousands of years before Adam"; he describes them as being "of various shapes; having the forms of serpents, scorpions, lions, wolves, jackals ... The Jinn are of three kinds; one on the land; one in the sea; and one in the air." They are capable of both good and evil: in one of Lane's translations of *The Thousand and One Nights,* the djinn is an enormous creature with a drawn sword determined to avenge himself on the merchant who has accidentally killed his son; in another, the envious brothers of a prosperous merchant plot to kill him and take over his possessions, only to be foiled by the merchant's wife, who turns into a djinn and rescues her husband.

Djinns are also known to call out a person's name and, if asking for admittance to their house, to knock twice—but never three times. From the Arabic meaning an intelligent spirit, the word is related to genie, that well-known magical creature who lives in bottles or lamps and grants wishes to those who release it.

Domovoy

From the Russian meaning "one of the household," this is a usually benevolent Slavic spirit who watches over the well-being of a family home. *Usually* benevolent, that is, but prone to fits of anger that mean he must be appeased. Appeasement may involve something as simple as offering the domovoy the remains of a meal, but in severe cases a household may have to resort to sacrificing a cock at midnight and sprinkling the corners of the house and yard with the bird's blood. Although the domovoy usually takes the form of a little old man, he may sometimes have diminutive horns and a tail, and in some cultures is depicted as a snake.

The 2008 Russian thriller movie *Domovoy* (translated as *The Ghost*) takes this creature's unpredictability several steps further. In it, the ghost acts as a sort of FAMILIAR (see page 74) to an author with writer's block, and becomes a particularly amoral contract killer, eventually turning his malevolence on the writer himself. A long way from the benevolent but touchy household god of the earlier myth ...

Draconian

In the early days of democracy in ancient Athens—around the seventh century BCE—a politician called Draco (whose name, aptly enough, means dragon) revised the city's system of laws radically, efficiently, and fairly. The problem was that his attitude to fairness meant that he viewed all crimes equally—and equally seriously—so that almost anything could be punishable by death, from fraud to stealing a cabbage. Hence the modern word "draconian," derived from Draco, which means extremely harsh and severe. It's normally applied to punishments, regulations, or the people who impose them, as in this summary, in a 2017 interview, by American author Alexander Weinstein of the horrors of modern life:

> *We shuffle out of office buildings after being laid-off by draconian bosses; we sit on hold for ten minutes only to be told by a supervisor that the charge on our cable bill can't be removed; we click a crying emoji on Facebook as our last whimper of protest.*

Ectoplasm

From Greek words meaning "forming cells on the outside," this is the sticky, half-liquid, half-solid substance that supposedly emanates from the body of a MEDIUM (see page 153) in a trance; according to a *Daily Mail* report dated 1923 it was cold to the touch, "comparable to contact with a reptile." It's also said to be gauze-like, so that it can drape over the medium's form like a veil. Sir Arthur Conan Doyle, creator of Sherlock Holmes but also a keen believer in SPIRITUALISM (see page 217), described in his last work, *The Edge of the Unknown* (1930), various attempts to prove scientifically the existence of ectoplasm. There were so many fraudulent spiritualists about that he was worried lest the genuine ones be tarred with the same brush and "indiscriminate disgrace should fall upon the human hyena with his material muslin and the true medium in trance clad in ectoplasmic drapery."

Eidolon

A word of Greek origin meaning a phantom, an apparition, an insubstantial image, sometimes written as "idolon" and related etymologically to "idol." It can designate a perfect, idealized example of something, as in the American magician and scholar Lee Siegel's description of a maharaja that he encountered in India:

> ... *an anachronistic, though thoroughly self-confident, aristocrat, an eidolon of grandeur in and for squalid times.*

But an eidolon can also be darker, more ESOTERIC (see page 70) than that, as Edgar Allan Poe revealed in his poem "Dreamland," published in 1844:

> *By a route obscure and lonely,*
> *Haunted by ill angels only,*
> *An Eidolon, named NIGHT,*
> *On a black throne reigns upright ...*

The dreams evoked in the poem involve a swamp "where the toad and newt encamp"; "dismal tarns and pools" inhabited by GHOULS (see page 85); and melancholy nooks where "... the traveler meets aghast/Sheeted Memories of the Past." It all suggests that Poe's "eidolon named Night" is a very gloomy creature indeed.

Eldritch

Weird, uncanny, ghostly, unnatural—this is a word with lots of strange connotations and no known etymology. It may be connected with elves ...

Early uses are mostly Scottish, notably this one by the poet Robert Burns (1759–96):

> *By some auld, houlet-haunted biggin,*
> *Or kirk deserted by its riggin,*
> *It's ten to ane ye'll find him snug in*
> *Some eldritch part,*
> *Wi' deils, they say,*
> *Lord save's! colleaguin*
> *At some black art.*

This is Burns at his most obscure, but it roughly means that you'll find the unearthly being (described in the previous verse) in an owl-haunted house, deserted church, or other eerie place, cozying up to devils and practicing some dark art.

The Scots don't have a monopoly on the word, however: it crossed the Atlantic in time to be picked up by Nathaniel Hawthorne, whose 1850 novel *The Scarlet Letter* has a little girl, annoyed because she's not allowed to pluck a rose from the nearby rose bushes, give "an eldritch scream." There's no suggestion here of any link with the Devil, but clearly the child has powerful lungs and is used to getting her own way.

Elf-lock

A tangled lock of hair, so named because it was said to be caused by elves mischievously twining hair (or sometimes horses' manes) in the night. Mercutio in Shakespeare's *Romeo and Juliet* (1590s) has a long speech about Queen Mab, whom he calls "the fairies' midwife": she gallops through the night, causing lovers to dream of love and lawyers to dream of fees. "This is that very Mab," he continues,

> *That plats the manes of horses in the night;*
> *And bakes the elf-locks in foul sluttish hairs,*
> *Which, once untangled, much misfortune bodes.*

The name was later given to a rare and apparently untreatable condition also known as Polish plait or *Plica polonica,* characterized by matting of the hair, which often becomes entangled in a sticky, moist mass. A paper published in 1964 by the Institute of British Geographers on the rather niche subject of "The Reclamation of Swamp in Pre-Revolutionary Russia" cites "ague or malarial fever and elflock" as being widespread in Poles'ye, an area of Eastern Europe encompassing parts of Ukraine, Belarus, and Poland.

Elf-shot

Suffering from some inexplicable affliction, as if you'd been shot by an elf. It's originally a Scottish term, often applied to livestock, but the lexicographer Susie Dent draws it into the twenty-first century in her novel *Guilty by Definition*, when two of the characters—lexicographers themselves—are trying to explain how a former colleague had always managed to make them feel inferior without being overtly rude:

> *"You came away feeling ..."*
> *"Elf-shot," Alex finished. "A conversation with Charlie left you with tiny wounds dealt by invisible archers, and they festered."*

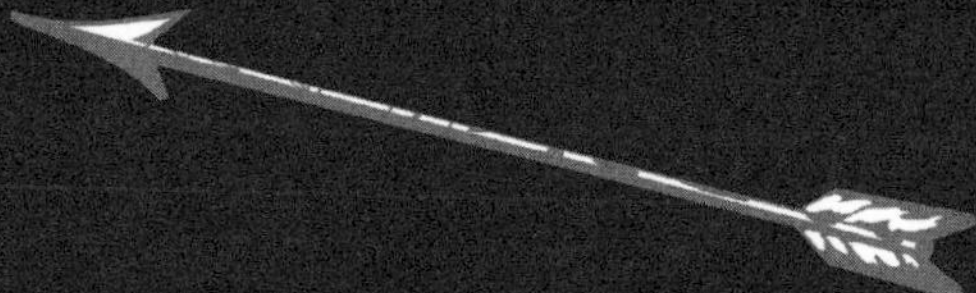

Erebus

The Greek god of darkness, son of Chaos, and brother of Night. His name is also given to a region of the Underworld, described by the Roman poet Virgil as "the lowest depths of gloom"; in Homer's *Iliad* it is the place where the Erinyes or FURIES (see page 79), goddesses of vengeance, live. The name comes from the Greek for darkness and the word is used to epitomize the darkest reaches of anything, be it a place or an emotion: in Shakespeare's *Merchant of Venice* (c. 1596), one of the young lovers, wooing his beloved against a background of romantic music, ponders the idea of a man who has "no music in himself." Such a man, he opines:

> *Is fit for treasons, stratagems, and spoils;*
> *The motions of his spirit are dull as night,*
> *And his affections dark as Erebus.*
> *Let no such man be trusted.*

Ergotism

Ergot is a disease of rye and other grasses caused by a hard fungus that looks like the spur on a cock's leg (the French for this sort of spur is *argot*, hence the English name). Ergot can also mean the seed of these grasses used medicinally, particularly to help strengthen contractions during childbirth. However, excessive use can cause convulsions and, because ergot restricts blood supply to the extremities, gangrene. There have been epidemics of ergotism—as this affliction is called—throughout history, and it has often been seen as a sign of demonic possession; some believe it was responsible for the convulsions experienced by the so-called "witches of Salem" in Massachusetts in the 1690s.

Ergotism is sometimes also known as St Anthony's Fire, because the medieval monks of the Order of St Anthony made a specialty of treating sufferers from the disease.

Erzulie

See Lwa (page 143).

Esoteric

From a Greek word meaning "inner," this means, in its strictest sense, intended for and intelligible to only a well-informed or initiated minority; the opposite is the less frequently used exoteric, which means open to and understandable by anyone. The nineteenth-century spiritualist Helena Blavatsky is quoted as saying that the so-called Secret Doctrine, a "synthesis of Science, Religion, and Philosophy" about which she wrote an influential book:

> *... is the common property of the countless millions of men born under various climates, in times with which History refuses to deal, and to which esoteric teachings assign dates incompatible with the theories of Geology and Anthropology.*

More loosely "esoteric" has come to mean abstruse, difficult to understand, and esoterica are esoteric objects or details. In this broader context, of course, what passes for esoterica can change rapidly: a 1958 edition of the *Spectator* magazine informed readers that in Soho it was usually possible to find "esoterica such as mangoes [and] passionfruit," a remark that couldn't have foreseen the wide range of tropical fruit that is available in London grocery stores today.

See also ARCANE (page 14).

Exorcist

A belief in demonic possession is a feature of many cultures and using prayer or other rituals to overcome it was common in Britain until the beginning of the seventeenth century. The practice has a powerful Christian lineage: a story told in the New Testament gospel of Matthew has Jesus casting out demons from two men who were possessed and "exceeding fierce"; at their request he sends the demons into a nearby herd of swine, who promptly run down a cliff into the sea and drown.

One way to "cure" someone who is apparently possessed is to perform an exorcism. The root of this word lies in the Greek for an oath, so to exorcize is to use an oath or holy name or spell to call out and drive away an evil spirit. An exorcist is the priest or pseudo-priest who performs this rite, as made universally famous in the 1973 movie of that name (and the novel by William Peter Blatty on which it is based). In this cinematic production, the exorcism of a young girl said to be possessed by a demon is achieved only by the priest taking the demon into his own body and killing himself.

Not all exorcisms are as extreme as this. See SHAMAN (page 204) for less violent forms of possession.

Faire Chlaidh

For many centuries in the Highlands of Scotland, every churchyard had an official known as "the watcher of the graves"—*faire chlaidh* (pronounced approximately "fairy claid") in Gaelic. The strange aspect of this post was that it was filled by the spirit of the person who had most recently been buried in that particular churchyard; when another burial took place, the incumbent was released from their duties and the newcomer took over.

In parts of England and Scandinavia, the watcher over the cemetery was known as a grim, or church grim, and often took the form of (the spirit of) a large black dog. The grim's role was to protect a new churchyard not only from thieves and vandals, but also from witches and the Devil. Unlike the *faire chlaidh*, the grim had no replacement lined up: the job was in perpetuity—hence the introduction of a dog or other non-human creature, so that a human soul was not condemned to it for all eternity.

The modern word "grim," an adjective meaning fierce, stern, forbidding, also once had a noun form, meaning both fierceness or anger and a frightening creature, and it's presumably this meaning that led to its being applied to the guardian of the graveyard.

Familiar

In its most widely used sense, "familiar" is an adjective etymologically related to "family" and means well known, easily recognized: a familiar face belongs to someone you know; a familiar argument is one you've heard before. As a noun, however, a familiar—sometimes known as a familiar spirit—is a supernatural creature, usually in animal form, who acts as a companion/assistant to a witch or other such magical being. The Old Testament warns against them: the Book of Leviticus cautions (in the words of the King James Version of 1611):

> *A man also or woman that has a familiar spirit, or that is a wizard, shall surely be put to death.*

Some later translations of the Bible are less specific: the New International Version (1973) refers to "A man or woman who is a medium or spiritist," while the English Standard Version (2001) has "A man or a woman who is a medium or a necromancer." They should still all be put to death, though.

Not every culture is so prescriptive, however; the American anthropologist Joan Halifax, writing about shamanism (see SHAMAN, page 204) among the indigenous Australians as recently as 1980, recorded two instances of familiars or doctor spirits enabling their human companions to effect cures: in both cases the familiars traveled in pairs, one duo taking the form of a little boy and a little girl, the other of two opossums, but both equally skilled and equally benevolent.

See also GRAYMALKIN (page 92).

Fetish

Although the word is of mixed European origin (part French, part Dutch, part Portuguese), the idea comes from West Africa and means an amulet or charm used by that region's Indigenous peoples, who believed it had magic powers. Early European travelers found that fetishes could be made from anything from straw to gold, and were most often hung around a person's neck to keep them safe while traveling.

By the nineteenth century, those European travelers, and their American counterparts, had taken the word home with them and used it to describe anything for which someone had an obsession. The historian Goldwin Smith—British born and educated, but later a teacher at Cornell University in New York State—wrote in 1867 of the Anglo-Irish politician Edmund Burke, a man known for his fervent beliefs on many subjects:

> *He was a worshipper of constitutional monarchy: it was his Fetish. He loved and adored it with the passionate loyalty which, as an Irishman in his own country, he would have felt towards the chief of his clan.*

Then, by the end of the century, psychologists had taken control of the word and linked it to unconventional and obsessive sexual behavior, in which desire was stimulated by "some article of wearing apparel, a lock of hair, etc.," as the American neurologist Landon Carter Gray wrote in 1893. So, although a fetish began with circlets of straw in the depths of West Africa, today it is more likely to refer to a longing to see your sexual partner dressed in leather.

See also GRIS-GRIS (page 96) and OBI (page 175).

Fith-fath

In medieval England, this was a human figure molded from wax or clay to resemble a particular individual. By sticking pins or nails into it, you could bring about a desired effect on the person concerned. One notorious case involved the future King James I of England who, in 1590, as James VI of Scotland, traveled to Denmark to marry the Danish king's sister Anne. James was notoriously hostile towards witches (see DEMONOLOGY, page 57) and the story goes that a certain Scottish coven used a fith-fath as part of the spells that conjured up a storm at sea, hoping that the king would be shipwrecked and drowned. The storm certainly happened, but the royal party managed to survive and the ensuing North Berwick witch trials clamped down remorselessly on the alleged perpetrators of the attack, with numerous so-called witches being tortured and executed.

Not all fith-faths are malevolent: they can also be used as amulets to protect travelers on a journey. The word comes from the Gaelic for SHAPE-SHIFTING (see page 205), and the idea seems to be that if you take on the appearance of, say, a deer, you disguise yourself from your enemies.

Formication

From the Latin for ant, this is the eerie sensation that ants are creeping over your skin. It is a recognized medical phenomenon: a treatise on *The Epidemics of the Middle Ages* by the German academic Justus Hecker, translated into English in 1884, contains a section on the deadly "sweating sickness," in the early stages of which many patients complained of "a disagreeable *creeping sensation or formication on their hands and feet*" which developed into "pricking pains, and an exceedingly painful sensation under the nails."

The concept isn't confined to Europe: see YUPUTKA (page 264).

Freischütz

In German myth, Freischütz is famed for his marksmanship. He makes a pact with the Devil, who gives him seven magic bullets, six of which are guaranteed to hit the target of Freischütz's choice, while the seventh must be aimed wherever the Devil dictates. *Freischütz* translates as "free shooter," though the "free" element seems odd given the context and has caused a great deal of discussion. One suggestion is that it means enchanted or controlled by the Devil, and therefore not free at all.

The various versions of Freischütz's story have one thing in common: they all end badly, the most frequent outcome being that the young marksman contrives to kill his fiancée on the eve of their wedding. The composer Carl von Weber gave this a happier twist in his 1821 opera *Freischütz*: the bullet seems about to hit the fiancée but is deflected and instead kills her rejected lover, who had persuaded Freischütz to cast the magic bullets in the first place. There are still penalties to be paid, though: you don't get off scot-free in tales like this.

For another example of it being foolish to enter into a pact with the Devil, see MEPHISTOPHELEAN (see page 154).

Furies

In Greek mythology these are a trio of goddesses, Alecto, Tisiphone, and Megaera, also known as the Eumenides or Erinnyes; their task is to punish crimes, particularly when the perpetrators have "escaped or defied public justice," according to Thomas Bulfinch. He describes them as having heads wreathed with serpents, and adds that their whole appearance was "terrific and appalling," so much so that when the tragic playwright Aeschylus, writing in the fifth century BCE, portrayed them as a chorus of fifty performers, then:

> *... the terror of the spectators was such that many fainted and were thrown into convulsions, and the magistrates forbade a like representation for the future.*

Erinyes seems to be a Latin translation of the Greek for fury, while *Eumenides* is surely the most euphemistic of euphemisms: it means "gracious goddesses," from a Greek word for well-disposed or friendly, though it seems abundantly clear that Alecto, Tisiphone, and Megaera were nothing of the sort. As for the name Furies, it came to us from Latin via French and emerged into English in the fourteenth century, about the same time as "fury," meaning a wild rage, a frenzy; sometimes even one that indicated a person was possessed by demons.

Gargoyle

Once upon a time, a dragon-like monster called La Gargouille lived in a cave near the river Seine at Rouen and emerged to swallow ships, breathe fire, and spout so much water from its mouth that it flooded the surrounding area. (In another version of the story, it lay across the river like a dam and flooded Rouen itself.) In an attempt to appease the monster, the townsfolk fed it a convicted criminal once a year, but it continued to wreak havoc until a seventh-century priest now known as St Romain successfully performed an EXORCISM (see page 71) and reduced it to ashes.

For many centuries after this—and particularly with the rise of Gothic architecture in the twelfth century—any building of substance was adorned with gargoyles, named in honor of the deceased dragon. The gargoyles' purpose was a harmless one: to drain water off a roof and steer it away from the walls of the building to prevent erosion. But they were frequently carved in the form of a GROTESQUE (see page 97)—fantastical figures in the shape of mythical animals or distorted human forms, with the water pouring out of their mouths onto the ground (and the passers-by) below. Because they took the form of living creatures, the suggestion arose that part of their role was to protect the building (which was often a church) from evil influences.

Then in the 1990s came an animated television series called *The Gargoyles*, in which a group of stone-carved creatures come alive at night to act as self-appointed vigilantes in New York. They shouldn't really have been called gargoyles—there's no water-spouting involved—but they were, and the idea of the gargoyles' protective role gained purchase as a result.

The word comes from the Old French for an animal's throat, with perhaps also a connection to the sound of gargling.

Gehenna

Hell or any similar place of torment. The name comes from "the valley of the son of Hinnom," which is just outside Jerusalem and features in the Old Testament Book of Jeremiah as a place where the people have been worshipping a false god (see BEELZEBUB, page 25). As punishment, God threatens them with unimaginable horrors, including forcing them to eat their own children, and claims that "every one that passeth thereby shall be astonished and hiss because of the plagues therein." On a similarly cheerless note, in *Paradise Lost*, Milton refers to "the pleasant valley of Hinnom" being turned into "black Gehenna ... the type of Hell," but the term can also refer to a more worldly horror: PG Wodehouse's comic novel *The Girl on the Boat* (1922) describes a particularly dreary South Coast resort as "this ozone-swept Gehenna."

Ghastly

Nowadays this is a word we use loosely, to mean dreadful or awful (both of them, come to think of it, words that used to be more powerful than they are now). They've all degenerated to mean nothing more eerie than "very bad" or "completely unenjoyable." But etymologically "ghastly" is related to "ghostly" (see GHOST, page 84) and derives from an Old English word meaning spirit. In early use it meant "causing terror," but soon (by the sixteenth century) developed into "deathly pale, like a ghost or a corpse." In Samuel Taylor Coleridge's "The Rime of the Ancient Mariner" (1798), the mariner has brought a curse on his ship and all his shipmates have died; he wakes from a sort of dream to find they have somehow been brought to life again and are about to go back to work:

The mariners all 'gan work the ropes,
Where they were wont to do:
They raised their limbs like lifeless tools—
We were a ghastly crew.

The loosely related "aghast" used to be a verb meaning to terrify but is now mostly employed as an adjective meaning overcome with horror. In a speech against American involvement in the 1960s war in Vietnam, the civil rights activist Martin Luther King Junior demanded that "somehow this madness must cease" and went on to express his revulsion at the situation: "I speak as a citizen of the world, for the world as it stands aghast at the path we have taken."

Ghost

According to the *Collins English Dictionary*, this is "the disembodied spirit of a dead person, supposed to haunt the living as a pale or shadowy vision." This has been the primary meaning for several hundred years, but the older idea of the word being synonymous with "spirit" or "soul" lingers in the expression "to give up the ghost," meaning to die or (in the case of an antiquated machine) to break down beyond hope of repair; and in the Holy Ghost, now more usually called the Holy Spirit, the third part (after God the Father and God the Son) of the Christian Holy Trinity.

The word "ghost" is derived from early Germanic words to do with fear and being frightened, which evolved to mean spirit (see GHASTLY, page 83); it is related to the German *Zeitgeist,* "the spirit of the time." Today, it has various other meanings suggestive of being hard to see: "the ghost of a smile" is a brave attempt at a smile, but not really a smile at all; while a ghostwriter is someone who does the actual work of writing—a celebrity's memoir, perhaps—but doesn't have their name splashed across the book's cover.

Ghoul

Tracing its origins back to an Arabic word for a SHAPE-SHIFTING (see page 205) desert demon, this is an evil spirit that steals corpses from the grave and eats them. European travelers discovered this legend in the eighteenth century; the word then came into English via French and was soon being used more loosely: by the mid-nineteenth century the novelist William Makepeace Thackeray was writing about "ghouls feasting on the fresh corpse of a reputation." Today if you describe someone as ghoulish you're likely to mean that they take a morbid delight in unpleasant things, such as malicious gossip or gory horror movies, rather than that they eat dead bodies.

Glossolalia

From the Greek for "speaking with tongues," this is the ability—supernatural or as a result of religious ecstasy—to speak and understand languages that you haven't learned. It happens in the New Testament Book of Acts, when the apostles are all gathered together:

> *And suddenly there came from heaven a sound like a mighty rushing wind, and it filled the entire house where they were sitting. And divided tongues as of fire appeared to them and rested on each one of them. And they were all filled with the Holy Spirit and began to speak in other tongues as the Spirit gave them utterance.*

Later in the New Testament, when St Paul is writing to the Corinthians, he lists the gift of tongues as one of many that may be granted by the Holy Spirit:

> *... to one is given through the Spirit the utterance of wisdom, and to another the utterance of knowledge according to the same Spirit ... to another the working of miracles, to another prophecy, to another the ability to distinguish between spirits, to another various kinds of tongues, to another the interpretation of tongues.*

It's by no means an exclusively Christian phenomenon, however: instances of people speaking in unknown languages occur in writings from ancient Greece to modern-day SHAMANISM (see page 204). The idea also overlaps with the paranormal concept of xenoglossy or xenoglossia (from the Greek for "foreign tongue"), in which a person under hypnosis reveals a knowledge of a language they haven't learned in their "normal" life. Whatever you choose to call it, it is hard to explain in non-spiritual, day-to-day terms.

Goety

A now obsolete word that meant much the same as NECROMANCY (see page 167)—a form of magic involving evil spirits and the dead. It comes from the Greek for a SORCERER (see page 215) and may be connected with another Greek term meaning "to wail." As a seventeenth-century translator of *The City of God*, a fifth-century philosophical work by St Augustine of Hippo, put it:

> *Goetie worketh upon the dead by invocation, so called of the noise that the practicers hereof make about graves.*

Golem

According to legend, a sixteenth-century rabbi named Judah Loew, living in Prague, created a clay figure and, by placing a magic word known as a *shem* in its mouth, brought it to life. The figure, known as a golem, was very strong and able to protect its master and the Jewish ghetto from Christian violence. But one day, it lost its temper and began smashing buildings, flinging boulders, and uprooting trees. Seeing that his creation was turning into a monster, the rabbi pulled the *shem* from its mouth so that the golem crumbled into dust. Loew was rabbi at what is now called the Old New Synagogue in Prague, where some believe the golem's dusty remains are still hidden away in the attic and where Loew's seat, to the right of the altar, has remained empty as a sign of respect ever since his death in 1609.

There have been many retellings of the golem story, some by Christians using it to criticize the Jews, but the most famous is a satirical version by the late-nineteenth-century Yiddish writer I.L. Peretz. In this, the Jews beg the rabbi to deactivate the golem on the basis that if it carries on along its destructive course there won't be any Gentiles left to heat the Sabbath ovens or to take down the Sabbath lamps (tasks that the Jews would have been forbidden to perform on their day of rest). Some twenty years later, the Austrian Gustav Meyrink came up with the horror novel *The Golem*, in which the title character is a ghostly creature who haunts the alleys of Prague and is seen as an incarnation of the ghetto itself.

Fast-forward a century or so and you find golems in Minecraft games and as a Pokemon character. So from being a concept that was intended to bring Jewish mystics closer to God and to protect people from persecution, the golem has, over the years, picked up shades of Frankenstein's monster and the *Phantom of the Opera*, to emerge in the twenty-first century as a creature (in Pokemon at least) that can fly at Mach speeds and fire energy-beams. Nevertheless, if you believe I.L. Peretz, the real golem still lurks in that synagogue attic in Prague, covered in cobwebs that will kill anyone who dares to touch them.

The word itself comes into English from Hebrew via German and means "shapeless matter." Like human beings, the golem is incomplete in God's eyes, emerging from clay and returning to dust. And, in this case, cobwebs.

Golgotha

"The place of skulls," from Aramaic, the language traditionally spoken by Christ. Golgotha was the name of the place outside the walls of Jerusalem where Christ was crucified. Rendered into Latin and then into English, the same word becomes Calvary. Strangely, though, Golgotha has come to be used for any sort of burial place—the eighteenth-century architect John Gwynn, one of the founders of the Royal Academy of Arts, wrote critically of the fact that Westminster Abbey had not been intended to be "a mere Golgotha for the Remains of the ... Dead." Calvary, on the other hand, can mean any place of great suffering: the Victorian novelist George Eliot, in her poem *A College Breakfast Party*, satirized the Church of England as "A Calvary where Reason mocks at Love."

It's interesting that one version of the word should focus on the dead, while the other concerns itself with the unhappiness of the living.

Gorgon

More monsters from Greek mythology (see Furies, page 79), the Gorgons were, again according to Thomas Bulfinch, "monstrous females with huge teeth like those of swine, brazen claws, and snaky hair"; the name comes for the Greek for "terrible." The most famous of the Gorgons was Medusa, said to be so ugly that anyone who looked directly at her would be turned to stone. This had been the fate of so many people and animals that she clearly had to be disposed of; the hero Perseus solved the problem by borrowing a shield from the goddess Athena and looking only at Medusa's reflection in the shield while he chopped her head off.

As with many terms referring to monsters (see leviathan, page 136, for another), the word has evolved from the specific to the general, in this case to denote any terrifying and/or ugly woman. In Oscar Wilde's 1894 comedy *The Importance of Being Earnest,* the hero Jack Worthing uses it to describe the formidable woman who is soon to become his mother-in-law:

> *Never met such a Gorgon … I don't really know what a Gorgon is like, but I am quite sure that Lady Bracknell is one. In any case, she is a monster, without being a myth, which is rather unfair …*

Grand Guignol

Named after a theater in Montmartre, Paris, which translates as "the great puppet," Grand Guignol meant, in the early twentieth century, a sensational style of drama performed there. The early examples focused on social commentary and the abuses to which the working classes were subject but, when the theater changed hands in 1898, the new owner introduced a sexual content intended to horrify and titillate in equal measure. There was no element of the supernatural in these plays: rather, they showed all the baser aspects of human nature and featured mad scientists, necrophiliacs, and serial killers. It's said that the management judged the success of each piece by how many audience members fainted and had to be carried out of the theater.

As a result, although the theater itself closed in 1962, the term has been adopted into English to describe anything gory, macabre, sensational, and (most importantly) over the top. It's often used by theater and cinema critics and in recent years has been applied to Stephen Sondheim's *Sweeney Todd,* about the Demon Barber who cuts his customers' throats; a scene from Puccini's opera *La Fanciulla del West*, in which blood drips through the ceiling after someone has been shot in an upstairs room; and a play in which a young boy unknowingly collects a severed head in a plastic bag.

Graymalkin

"When shall we three meet again?" may be the most famous opening line in Shakespeare, spoken by one of the witches in *Macbeth* (1606). The three are arranging to get together to accost Macbeth and give him the prophecies that cause all the trouble; but for the moment they have other places to go, other people to see. "I come, Graymalkin!" cries one of them, answering a summons that the rest of us haven't heard, calling her away.

This is the only mention Graymalkin gets in the play, so we are left to assume that the witch is going to join her cat FAMILIAR (see page 74); Grimalkin, the usual spelling, was a name given to a cat, particularly an elderly female one, and hence became a disparaging term for an elderly woman. "Malkin" on its own is an old word for a slovenly woman, and the longer term almost certainly comes from the color gray. Etymologically, there is nothing ARCANE (see page 14) about it, though its witchy associations are SINISTER (see page 208) enough.

Gremlin

Not a medieval sprite or troublemaker in the mold of an elf or a TROLL (see page 234), this is a twentieth-century invention, dating only from the early days of the Royal Air Force. Originally used to mean a lowly menial, it had become, by the onset of the Second World War, a slang term for the imaginary beings who caused mystifying trouble: "weird little creatures who fly about looking for unfortunate pilots who are either lost or in difficulties with the weather" (according to Pauline Gower, an early female aviator, in her memoir *Women with Wings,* 1938) or "awful little people ... who run up and down the wing with scissors going 'snip, snap, snip'" (travel writer Charles Graves, *The Thin Blue Line,* 1941). The gremlins of Roald Dahl's 1943 book of that name were also associated with the RAF, but within a year of its publication the multi-volume *American Speech*, published by the American Dialect Society, was able to observe that the gremlin "seems to be extending its sphere of operations, so that the term can be applied to almost anything that inexplicably goes wrong in human affairs."

Why is it called a gremlin? It's been suggested that the word is related to "goblin," but—appropriately enough for something whose actions are inexplicable—no one seems to be certain.

Grim

See FAIRE CHLAIDH (page 73).

Grimoire

Nothing to do with "grim," etymologically this is more closely related to "grammar" and means a textbook. Not just any textbook, however: specifically, one associated with magic. Although the word itself has been in use in English only from the nineteenth century, when it was adopted from French, books of spells of various kinds in various cultures date back thousands of years. Their contents vary wildly: one of the earliest grimoires to have come down to us is attributed (almost certainly wrongly) to a medieval Pope, Honorius III (1150–1227), and contains instructions for saying a Mass; some go to the other extreme, explaining how to enter into a pact with the Devil but also, in some instances, suggesting ways of getting one over on the evil spirits that your spells might have evoked. In her 2024 book *The Way Through the Woods*, Rebecca Beattie, who describes herself as a green witch, cites a ritual from an earlier grimoire which promotes commitment in a new relationship. It involves an apple, a few hairs from the heads of the couple involved, and initials written in blood on a piece of parchment, though Beattie's modern adaptation dispenses with the blood (and indeed the parchment) and creates a romantic atmosphere using candles and incense.

In modern witchcraft, which tends to be more earth- and nature-loving and less concerned with the forces of evil than its medieval predecessors, a grimoire may be passed down from mother to daughter like a recipe book and contain healing potions and advice on promoting harmony in your relationships, both with others and with the planet. And, just as with a recipe book, where you may choose to ignore anything too complicated or anything with coriander in it, so with a grimoire you can adapt your magic—black, white, or green—to deal with your own particular concerns.

Gris-gris

Sometimes spelled gree-gree, greegree, or grigri, which is how it is pronounced, this is an amulet or charm in the form of a piece of paper kept in a bag. Originating (as both a concept and a word) in West Africa, it was transported during the slave trade to the Caribbean and southern parts of the United States. The original idea was that a gris-gris protected its owner from harm; later it was also used to harm others. The British explorer John Matthews, writing in 1788 about a journey to the river Sierra Leone (and using yet another spelling), was obviously intrigued by the charm's versatility:

> *Every griggory is assigned its particular office: one is to preserve him from shot, one from poison [etc.] ... and when a man happens to be killed ... they only say his griggory was not so good as the person's who occasioned his death.*

Some twenty years later, another British traveler to what is now Sierra Leone, Joseph Corry, wrote about the local gris-gris tree (*Erythrophleum suaveolens*), a species of mahogany also known as the ordeal tree. According to him, the "trial by red water," used to judge serious crimes, "consists in making the accused drink a quantity of water, into which is infused the poisonous juice of the melley or *gris-gris* tree." The judges, Corry observed, had generally decided on their verdict beforehand, with the result that:

> *If the unhappy object of suspicion is affected in such a manner as they consider as a proof of guilt, his brains are knocked out upon the spot, or the body is so inflated by the pernicious liquid that it bursts.*

So the gris-gris amulet was used for protection; the juice of the tree not so much.

See also ORDEAL (page 177).

Grotesque

Taken into English from French in the sixteenth century, this was originally a noun used in an architectural context to denote a carving that mixed human, animal, and plant forms in a distorted way; it quickly became an adjective to describe such a work. The French essayist Michel de Montaigne, writing in 1580 of the work of a painter he employed, said that the man completed the central portion of a picture with great care and skill, then filled the empty spaces around it with "grotesques, which are odd fantastic figures without any grace but what they derive from their variety, and the extravagance of their shapes."

It's easy to see how the idea of an "odd fantastic figure" moved away from architecture and into the wider world, so the word came to mean anything that was strangely distorted or bizarre, from a "grotesque monster" to a "grotesque turn of phrase" (one that was in bad taste or out of place). Charles Dickens—many of whose characters could be described as grotesque—portrayed the villainous Daniel Quilp in *The Old Curiosity Shop* (1841) as having restless and cunning eyes, a bristly unshaven chin, and also an unhealthy complexion:

> *But what added most to the grotesque expression of his face was a ghastly smile, which, appearing to be the mere result of habit and to have no connection with any mirthful or complacent feeling, constantly revealed the few discoloured fangs that were yet scattered in his mouth, and gave him the aspect of a panting dog.*

Not a man you wanted to meet in a dark alley at night. Or at any other time.

See GARGOYLE (page 81) for more about fantastic figures and GHASTLY (page 83) for how that word's meaning has evolved over the years.

Guising

Related to "disguise," this is an old Scottish word for masquerading, often used in the context of HALLOWE'EN (see page 102). In Peter May's 2010 detective novel *Freeze Frame*, set on an island off the coast of Brittany, the hero, convinced that he is being chased by a man he suspects of murder, is terrified to be confronted by "a human skull; a green face with black spots": this apparition turns out to be two teenage girls disguised as a skeleton and a witch. Their father—a Frenchman with a penchant for things Scottish—explains simply, "It's Hallowe'en, Monsieur Macleod. We're out guising" and invites him home for a malt whisky. The fact that he and his wife are disguised as Laurel and Hardy, "bowler hats above whitened faces," indicates that the key to guising—in Brittany, at least—is dressing up rather than necessarily embracing the Hallowe'en theme.

In fact, guising has been known in Scotland since the sixteenth century, although it was originally done at New Year, and can certainly be seen as a precursor of today's trick-or-treating.

See also TATTIE-BOGLE (page 227).

Gurumapa

A man-eating giant with long, prominent fangs, this is the Nepalese equivalent of KRAMPUS (see page 133) and the various other BOGEY-MEN (see page 31) reputed to kidnap naughty children. The story goes that a man named Kesh Chandra, exiled from his home for gambling away his property, had his last remaining food eaten by pigeons. The pigeons, seeing that he repented of his extravagance, took pity on him and their droppings mysteriously turned to gold. This treasure was too heavy for Kesh Chandra to carry, but at this point he encountered Gurumapa, and not only persuaded the giant not to eat him, but inveigled him into helping him carry the gold home. In return, Kesh Chandra allowed Gurumapa to live in his attic and also to carry off any children whose parents invoked him when the youngsters had been misbehaving.

After some years of this the parents agreed that enough was enough. Gurumapa was sent to live on Tundikhel, a large, grassy space now in the center of the Nepalese capital Kathmandu, but at that time out in the countryside. The giant's agreement to this arrangement came with a price, however: each year, at the time of the Hindu spring festival of Holi, people prepare a feast on Tundikhel to keep Gurumapa happy and prevent him from stealing any more children.

It's not clear what the name Gurumapa means, but the *guru* element is probably from the same Sanskrit source as the word used in modern English: a teacher or spiritual leader, someone deserving of respect.

Hag

Quite late on in Shakespeare's *Macbeth* (1606)—after the ghost of the murdered Banquo has appeared in the famous banqueting scene—the guilt-ridden Macbeth seeks out the witches who predicted that he would become king and thus set the entire tragedy in motion. Shakespeare uses the word "witch" only once in the course of the play—more often they are referred to as "the weird sisters," but here Macbeth addresses them by another name: "you secret, black, and midnight hags." He's interrupting them brewing up a CAULDRON (see page 43) full of "eye of newt," "toe of frog," and the like, and when he asks them what they are doing, the reply is the sinister "A deed without a name."

Macbeth's meaning of hag—a woman thought to have dealings with the Devil—is the oldest one, found in Middle English in the thirteenth century and related to old Dutch, German, and Scandinavian words for a sorceress; by the beginning of the fifteenth century it had been adopted into broader use, meaning an ugly old woman, not necessarily one with magical powers or demonic connections. But a couple of hundred years on it had become specific again and meant either a spirit (sometimes known as Old Hag) who visited sleeping people or animals and made them feel as if they were suffocating, or the feeling of suffocation itself. (For a variation on this idea, see NIGHTMARE, page 172).

Modern WICCA (see page 254) uses Hag (with a respectful initial capital) to mean the darkest aspect of what it venerates as the Triple Goddess, following MAIDEN (see page 148) and Mother; it represents the time in a woman's life when she has attained wisdom and the status of an elder within a group. That period is associated with autumn and winter but has the positive attribute that the Hag will be reborn as the Maiden when spring comes around again. In this context Hag and Crone are used interchangeably, though in common parlance a crone is also a witch-like old woman—the word's etymology connects it to "carrion," so a crone is likely to be frightening, if not actually flesh-eating.

To sum up, then: today's witchcraft, with its veneration of all things feminine, puts a positive slant on the Hag and the Crone; otherwise, they remain the scary old women, possibly with warts on their long, hooked noses, who haunted childhood stories.

Hallowe'en

Nowadays, this is the evening when children dress up as a GHOST (see page 84), skeletons, or Elphaba from *Wicked* to go out "trick-or-treating"; willing householders stock up on sweets and candies to hand out to anyone who comes knocking on the door. Pumpkins carved into the form of a JACK O' LANTERN (see page 125) adorn doorsteps, bonfires are lit, and firework displays organized. Brits who deplore the eclipsing of Guy Fawkes Day and complain that Hallowe'en is an American aberration should remember that Guy Fawkes became a public figure only in 1605, when he failed to blow up the Houses of Parliament; the traditions of Hallowe'en go back a long, long way before that and are very firmly rooted in the British Isles.

Literally "holy eve" or "the eve of All Hallows or All Saints Day," the name Hallowe'en—dating from the sixteenth century—originally denoted a Christian festival celebrated on October 31, and followed by two more holy days: All Saints' Day on November 1 and All Souls' Day on November 2. The Christian ritual was (like so many Christian celebrations) superimposed on a much older Celtic festival, SAMHAIN (see page 196); many of the Hallowe'en traditions, including the pumpkin-based one, went to the United States from the British Isles and can be traced back to Scotland's celebration of TATTIE-BOGLE (see page 227) and beyond.

As for the word itself, the apostrophe in Hallowe'en (indicating that the v is missing from "even," meaning evening or eve) seems never to have been standard: Robert Burns didn't use it in 1786, but his fellow Scot Walter Scott did in 1803. Today, the (originally Scottish) *Chambers Dictionary* holds out for it; Collins and the *Oxford English Dictionary* do not. So, you must choose between being teased for pedantry or mocked for slovenliness ...

Harpies

In Classical myth, according to Thomas Bulfinch, these were "disgusting birds with the heads of maidens, with long claws and faces pale with hunger." To these unappealing characteristics the Roman poet Virgil adds "a foul discharge." In Homer and other Classical Greek writers they appear as violent winds that carry people away; they also tormented a blind man called Phineus by either stealing or defiling any food that was put in front of him.

The name is taken from the Greek and today is used to mean a cruel and greedy woman, such as a certain "Amelia What'shername" in Virginia Woolf's *Mrs Dalloway* (1925), "handing round cups of tea punctually at five—a leering, sneering obscene little harpy."

Hecate

Sometimes spelled Hekate, this is a Greek deity whose name translates as "far-darting one." Associated with the moon, she is a goddess of crossroads that are traversed at night and thus more generally of witchcraft. She is often depicted as having three bodies and/or three heads, possibly because of her connection with crossroads (which in Latin is "trivia" or three ways).

As goddess of witchery, Hecate features in Shakespeare's *Macbeth* (1606), where she berates the three witches for having dared, without consulting her,

> ... *To trade and traffic with Macbeth*
> *In riddles and affairs of death.*

She also earns a mention in *A Midsummer Night's Dream* (c. 1595), when the fairy Puck talks of it being the time of night when graves open and each one "lets forth his sprite":

> *And we fairies, that do run*
> *By the triple Hecate's team*
> *From the presence of the sun,*
> *Following darkness like a dream,*
> *Now are frolic.*

And she crops up in *King Lear* (1605–6), when the king, as part of the speech in which he disowns his daughter Cordelia for not expressing unconditional love for him, calls on "the mysteries of Hecate and the night."

Other writers of that period invoke Hecate too, but Shakespeare's references show just how potent she was deemed to be, particularly around midnight and into the early hours (see WITCHING HOUR, page 258).

Hejkal

A forest demon of Czech folklore, normally found in human form, who camouflages himself with moss, leaves, ferns, and wood. Hejkal is renowned for his powerful screech (the name translates as "howler" or "yeller") and anyone trespassing in the woods who returns the demon's call may find that he has pounced onto their back; if he is really angry, he may tear them apart. Hejkal may sometimes be caught in traps that hunters have laid in the forest and is always grateful to anyone who releases him: they may be rewarded with the gift of special skills or even magical powers.

Hellhound

A word that means exactly what you would expect it to mean—a hound from Hell, or some malevolent being in the shape of a dog. It's been in the language since the time of Alfred the Great, the ninth century CE, and by the fourteenth it was also being used as a more general term of abuse, to mean any evil person, not necessarily one who had connections with the Devil or was in canine form. Sir Thomas More—the staunch Catholic who lost his head when he refused to recognize Henry VIII as head of the Church of England—straddled the two meanings when, in 1532, he wrote a diatribe against various prominent Protestants and referred, in modern spelling, to "Neither Luther, Tyndal, nor Huskin, nor all the hellhounds that the devil hath in his kennel."

Hemlock

Traditionally held to be the plant that poisoned the Greek philosopher Socrates—and other ancient Greeks who had been condemned to death—hemlock is a hardy herbaceous member of the carrot family which can boast not only that all parts of it are toxic, but that its hollow stems remain toxic for three years after the rest of the plant has died. As far back as the eighth century CE (1,200 years too late to be of any use to Socrates), its power had been harnessed so that it could be used medicinally—and in strictly limited doses—as a sedative.

Why it is called hemlock, no one seems to know. According to the *Oxford English Dictionary*, not only is it "of uncertain origin," but there are no related words in any other languages.

Henbane

"Bane" is used in modern English to mean something that causes great distress ("He's the bane of my existence"), but in earlier times it was more powerful still—it meant something that caused destruction or death. As a result, lots of plants have folk names that end in *-bane*. Wolfsbane (see MONKSHOOD, page 159) may once have been used to kill wolves, and there are dogbanes, ratsbanes, and even a leopard's bane, which one seventeenth-century writer described as having a root like a scorpion. Henbane, belonging to the genus *Hyoscyamus* and related to BELLADONNA (see page 27) and MANDRAKE (see page 151), comes in three varieties, black, white, and yellow, and has been known to be narcotic, and poisonous in larger doses, since at least the fourteenth century. There's some dispute as to whether or not the name comes from the effect the plant had on hens, but the *Oxford English Dictionary* does cite a 1475 source as saying that it will kill ducks.

This didn't stop henbane being—allegedly—a regular feature of witches' potions. The website gothichorrorstories.com suggests that it gave oracles their sight and also made witches fly (see BELLADONNA for more about that); it also quotes the experience of a nineteenth-century German nobleman called Gustav Schenk who reported that taking henbane initially induced physical discomfort, including giddiness, hammering pains in his head, and the sensation that his mirror was moving around in front of him so that he couldn't keep his face inside its frame. Schenk's physical symptoms soon gave way to something much more disturbing:

> *Above my head water was flowing, dark and blood-red. The sky was filled with herds of animals. Fluid, formless creatures emerged from the darkness. I heard words, but they were all wrong and nonsensical, and yet they possessed for me some hidden meaning.*

There is much more in the same vein, and nowhere is there any explanation of why Schenk chose to take enough henbane to produce this effect, but modern medicine (and the most rudimentary common sense) would discourage it.

Heretic

A word applied to anyone who holds religious opinions at variance with those of the Catholic Church or—more recently and more loosely—opinions that differ from those regarded as orthodox or acceptable, whether or not they are to do with religion. Its origins can be traced back to the Greek for "able to choose"—which is rather ironic, given that the ability to choose is precisely what the term condemns. The noun "heresy" (meaning heretical beliefs) has been around since the thirteenth century and "heretic" since the fourteenth, because in those days there seem to have been plenty of sects whose beliefs the Pope disapproved of; but use of both words really took off after 1534, when Henry VIII broke with the Catholic Church and declared himself head of the Church of England. In Catholic Europe both he and his Protestant daughter Elizabeth I were frequently described as heretics.

The more casual use dates back to at least 1600, when Shakespeare used it in *Much Ado About Nothing*: Don Pedro says to the confirmed bachelor Benedick, "Thou wast ever an obstinate heretic in the despite of beauty," meaning that he takes the unorthodox line of being indifferent to beautiful women. Nearly three centuries later the scientist T.H. Huxley, an early supporter of Charles Darwin's ideas on evolution, applied the idea to his own field: "It is the customary fate of new truths to begin as heresies and to end as superstitions."

Hex

To bewitch, specifically in a bad way: to put a hex on someone is to curse them, in order to bring them bad luck. The word comes from the German *Hexer*, a witch, and entered North American English via Pennsylvania Dutch (which isn't actually Dutch, but a mixture of various German—*Deutsch*—dialects). In the mid-nineteenth century *hex* meant a witch, acquiring its present meaning in the early twentieth century.

The word, from 1983, began to reach a whole new audience by becoming the name of the magic-powered, self-building computer at the Unseen University in Terry Pratchett's Discworld novels. Hex the computer has a number of unusual features: it can upgrade itself with extra cheese; its mouse really is a mouse (of the cheese-eating rodent variety); its memory storage facility is a beehive; it thinks it's alive; and can be very bad-tempered. Its name isn't entirely magical, though; it also takes punning advantage of another meaning of hex: an abbreviation for *hexadecimal,* an arithmetical system with sixteen rather than ten as its base, much used in computing.

Hobgoblin

One of many names for an evil or mischievous spirit, as embodied by Puck in Shakespeare's *A Midsummer Night's Dream* (c. 1595). One of the fairies in the play, on encountering Puck, recognizes that he is "that shrewd and knavish sprite/Call'd Robin Goodfellow" and goes on to observe:

Those that Hobgoblin call you, and sweet Puck,
You do their work, and they shall have good luck.

The "hob" part of the name is a corruption of Rob (itself an abbreviation of Robin, as in Robin Goodfellow) and was in use to mean *hobgoblin* by 1500, some thirty years before the longer word is first recorded. So to call someone Hobgoblin is a tautology—it's tacking a French-derived word for a mischievous sprite (goblin) on to the English one (hob). English folklore makes a distinction, though: a goblin tends to be ugly and malevolent; a hobgoblin is more fun.

Hocus-pocus

Today meaning trickery, chicanery, or mystifying jargon, this was first used in the seventeenth century to signify a juggler or conjuror, particularly one who performed at a fair or market. Thomas Ady, whose treatise on witchcraft, *A Candle in the Dark*, was published in 1656, mentions such a performer who apparently called himself:

> ... *The Kings Majesties most excellent Hocus Pocus ... because that at the playing of every Trick, he used to say, Hocus pocus, tontus talontus, vade celeriter jubeo, a dark composure of words, to blinde the eyes of the beholders, to make his Trick pass the more currantly without discovery, because when the eye and the ear of the beholder are both earnestly busied, the Trick is not so easily discovered.*

The magician's incantation may have sounded like Latin, but it was nothing of the sort—the words were made up to impress a credulous audience.

By the nineteenth century, when the American writer Washington Irving was traveling in Europe, hocus pocus was changing its meaning: observing the civil unrest in Spain in 1843, Irving described "the hocus-pocus of political affairs," which turned yesterday's rebels into today's ardent royalists. But a mere ten years later he was referring to a form of SÉANCE (see page 202) that had become all the rage in New York as "the hocus-pocus of moving tables"—much nearer the word's modern sense.

See also MUMBO-JUMBO (page 162).

Hodgepoke

Puck, or Robin Goodfellow, the mischievous sprite described under HOBGOBLIN (see page 112) has many alternative names, and this is one of them. It's not clear what it derives from, but hodge is an archaic form of Roger, used (in the manner of every Tom, Dick, and Harry or John Doe) as a general-purpose name for an unsophisticated rustic, while poke, related to puck, is yet another archaic word for a malicious spirit. It's possible that a combination of these two elements gave us an impish creature that flits around the countryside causing mayhem.

Hog reek

Hobgoblins (see page 112) and other creatures from the dark side are most likely to appear either at night or when the weather is turbulent. So in Scotland they could well be seen during a hog reek—"blinding and choking snow drifts driven by a gale," according to the online *Scottish National Dictionary*. The second part of the term comes from the Scots dialect word for smoke, which also gave Edinburgh its nickname of Auld Reekie; the origin of the first part isn't known, but there's no suggestion that it has anything to do with hogs, however tempting it may be to imagine a herd of swine emerging from a blinding snowdrift to wreak some sort of havoc.

Horripilation

From the Latin for "bristling hair," this is goose flesh—the sensation of having the hairs on your skin stand up on end, usually because of cold, fear, disgust, or, to use another metaphor, because something has "made your flesh creep." For an even less pleasant sensation, see formication (page 77).

Ichneumon

Pronounced *ick-new-mon*, this is a word from the Greek for a hunter or tracker and is the name of a creature alleged to be particularly adept at tracking down crocodile eggs. In modern zoology it is a real animal—the Egyptian mongoose, which feeds not only on eggs but on insects, birds, amphibians, and reptiles. It was known in Classical times, when the Greek geographer Strabo (writing in the first centuries before and after Christ) recorded that it attacked crocodiles basking in the sun by entering their open jaws and eating them, effectively, from the inside out. Some decades later, the Roman expert on natural history, Pliny the Elder, recorded the creature's way of protecting itself when preying on the venomous asp, with which he said it waged a "mortal war":

> *He often wallows in the Mud, and then dries himself again in the Sun; and when he hath thus armed himself with many skins, he goes forth to combat. In Fight he sets up his Tail and, turning it to the Enemy, receives all the Strokes [from the Asp] without harm, until he spies a Time to turn his Head on one Side, in order to catch the Asp by the Throat.*

Impressive for a creature weighing no more than 8¾lb (4kg).

But it is the period between Pliny and modern times that really interests us here, as sometime over the centuries the ichneumon gained a reputation as the mortal enemy not of the asp but of the dragon. Opinions vary as to how it manages to slay the much larger beast: creeping in through its nostrils is one version; waiting patiently until it can make a single fatal bite to the dragon's vulnerable neck is another. It must also have helped the ichneumon's campaign that it was legendarily immune to the murderous gaze of the BASILISK (see page 23). But however it managed it, this tiny carnivore has been widely credited for causing dragons to become extinct.

Ignis fatuus

The Latin for "foolish fire" and also known as "will-o'-the-wisp," this is in fact a phosphorescent light produced by gases that spontaneously combust over rotting vegetable matter in marshy ground. The "fire" appears to float above the ground at night and to recede when anyone approaches it, leading to the suggestion that it is the work of a mischievous sprite enticing mortals away from the path they intend to take and sometimes drowning them in the bog. The seventeenth-century satirist Samuel Butler, in his poem *Hudibras* (1663), wrote of:

> *An Ignis Fatuus, that bewitches,*
> *And leads men into Pools and Ditches.*

A third name for the phenomenon occurs in John Milton's poem *L'Allegro* (1645), which refers to someone being led by "Friar's lantern"—the "friar" perhaps being a malicious spirit in disguise, seeming to help the traveler by carrying a light for them to follow, but in fact luring them farther and farther into the unknown ...

Imprecation

This comes from the Latin for "to pray," but it's a particularly unpleasant form of prayer: more a curse or malediction, a sort of spell intended to bring misfortune or disaster. It could be aimed at a ship that goes on to find itself in a sudden storm (see FITH-FATH, page 76) or perhaps at a person the imprecator wants to be sure of beating at cards. The English poet William Habington (1605–1654) used it in this context, in an elegy on the early death of Henry Campbell, son of the Earl of Argyll. Pondering why such an estimable young man should have lived only twenty years when so many evildoers last much longer, he wrote:

Why alive
Is yet disorder'd greatnesse, and all they
Who the loose lawes of their wilde blood obey?
Why lives the gamester, who doth blacke the night
With cheats and imprecations?

Incantation

Deriving ultimately from the Latin for "to sing," this has over the centuries come to be associated with magical rituals: it's a form of words, sung or chanted, and used as a spell. Percy Bysshe Shelley, in his 1819 *Ode to the West Wind*, uses the wind as a metaphor for a force that can bring desirable changes to society and begs it to:

Drive my dead thoughts over the universe
Like wither'd leaves to quicken a new birth!
And, by the incantation of this verse,

Scatter, as from an unextinguish'd hearth
Ashes and sparks, my words among mankind!

Just listen to me, in other words, and all will be well.

Incubus

From the same source as "incubate," an incubus can be traced back to a Latin word for "to lie upon" and indicates a male demon believed to visit women while they sleep to consort with them. It's implicit in the word that the incubus is on top—if the activity is the other way around and you are a man who finds a female demon underneath you, she is a succubus.

This concept was taken very seriously in the Middle Ages, notably in the *Malleus Maleficarum* or *Hammer of Witches*, published in 1487 and hugely influential for three hundred years as a casebook in witch trials. The book gives guidelines on what constitutes evidence and how torture and executions should be carried out when (almost inevitably) the accused is found guilty. It also considers at some length whether or not children can be conceived by an act of intercourse in which an incubus or a succubus is involved. "Probably not" is a much-simplified version of its conclusion.

Inexorable

Tracing its origins back to the Latin for "to pray," this is an adjective describing someone or something that will not be moved by any amount of praying: they are adamant, uncompromising, unyielding, relentless ... Towards the end of Shakespeare's *Romeo and Juliet* (c. 1595), Romeo, believing wrongly that Juliet is dead, is determined to break into her tomb and kill himself too. He instructs his servant not to pry into what he intends to do, nor to try to stop him:

> *The time and my intents are savage-wild,*
> *More fierce and more inexorable far*
> *Than empty tigers or the roaring sea.*

Inferno

Another word for Hell, this time with particular emphasis on the fact that condemned souls are burning there. It's an Italian word, used by the great poet Dante Alighieri as the title of the first part of his *Divine Comedy* (c. 1307–21), to be followed by *Purgatory* and *Paradise*. Later, an inferno could mean anything hellish—as when the Victorian scholar Thomas Carlyle, writing in 1839, waxed eloquent on the dreadful living conditions of the poor, who were condemned to "this black unluminous unheeded Inferno, and Prisonhouse of souls in pain." Alternatively, it can signify any enormous fire: according to *Newsweek*, reporting on fires in Kuwait during the First Gulf War of 1991: "The occupiers set 600 of the country's 950 oil wells ablaze, a smoky inferno that created dusk at noon." Today this is the most common sense of the word, but it may still apply to anything, fiery or not, that is overwhelming, unpleasant, and inescapable.

Initiation

Etymologically, this means nothing more sinister than "beginning"—it's related to "initial." But it's more frequently used for a secret ceremony or a gruelling test that an applicant must undergo before being admitted into some sort of society. This may mean nothing much more than a glorified dare, anything from shoplifting to pricking your finger to mingle your blood with that of fellow initiates and pledging your loyalty to them. Or it can be on an altogether higher plane: the Roman historian Plutarch, writing (in the second century CE) about what happened to the souls of "good men" after their death, suggested that they passed through various stages, from men to heroes to demi-gods, and finally ...

> *... after passing, as in the rite of initiation, through a final cleansing and sanctification, and so freeing themselves from all that pertains to mortality and sense, are thus ... elevated into gods, admitted thus to the greatest and most blessed perfection.*

Invultuation

Sometimes "invultation," this uncommon word can trace its origins back to the Latin for countenance or likeness and means the making of a likeness, particularly a wax figure, for the purposes of WITCHCRAFT (see page 256). The nineteenth-century English clergyman Samuel Maitland, in his essay *False Worship*, quotes an earlier Latin source as writing about "Sorcery ... by invocations of demons, by certain invultuations and other evil deeds"; that same source described an invultuor as "a magician who conjures up images for magical arts." According to Maitland there is more to the concept than making waxen figures: he refers also to "those who chanted, derided, and made obligatories of sacred or impious nocturnal rites." It's clearly a controversial and potentially alarming practice.

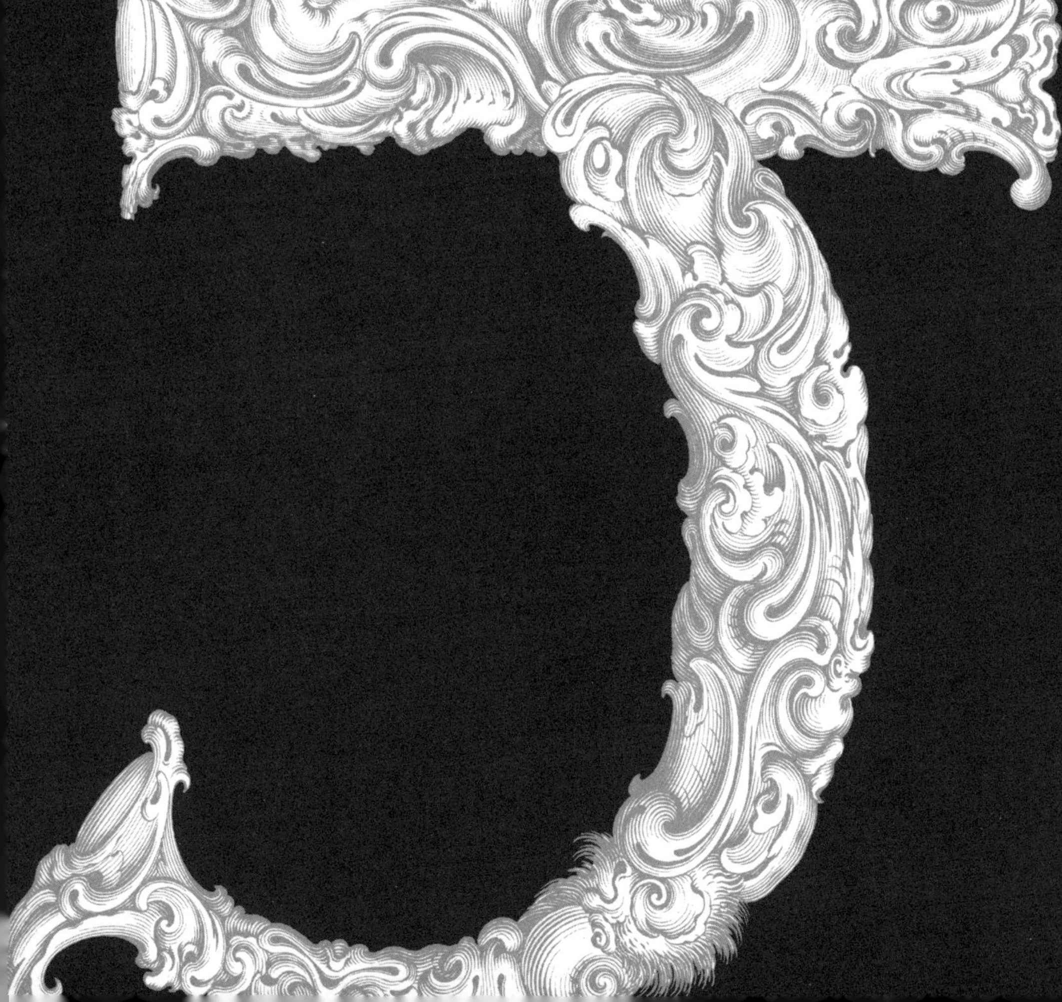

Jack o' lantern

Originally used as a synonym for IGNIS FATUUS (see page 118) or will o' the wisp, in the seventeenth century this term came—because of its connection with bright lights—to mean a nightwatchman who carried a lantern in order to light people's way. From there, initially in the United States, the Jack o' lantern became that quintessential Hallowe'en decoration, a hollowed-out pumpkin with the outline of a face carved into it and a candle or other light inside it. As *Boys Life*, the magazine of the Boy Scouts of America, put it in 1920: "Ain't no sort o' Hallowe'en lest we got a jack-o'-lantern."

In fact, although most Americans—and an ever-growing numbers of citizens of the rest of the world—would agree with that sentiment, the tradition of carving vegetables for Hallowe'en began not in the USA but in Scotland, and not with a pumpkin but with a turnip. See TATTIE-BOGLE (page 227).

Jigoku

The Japanese Buddhist term for Hell, or rather an all-embracing term for the many subdivisions of Hell, home to those whose sins make them ineligible for rebirth in any other realm. By some counts there are 64,000 different Hells, but in a simplified approach there are eight hot ones and eight cold, of which the hot are also designated the "great Hells." Each caters for a specific type of sinner and has its own style of punishment: Tokatsu Jigoku, "reviving Hell," for example, is reserved for those who kill without remorse. In a burning hot atmosphere, the souls fight each other to the death with iron clubs; as soon as one dies, it is revived and forced to fight all over again.

In Shugō Jigoku, "crushing Hell," killers who have also committed the sin of lechery perpetually climb trees with razor-sharp leaves, slicing themselves to pieces; there are two burning Hells, one ten times hotter than the other, reserved for those who have committed crimes against the Buddhist faith and Buddhist clergy; and a final, deepest Hell where sufferers are so hungry and thirsty that they tear apart their own bodies and drink their own blood in a desperate but unavailing attempt to satisfy their needs.

Even the worst of sinners are not condemned to Jigoku for eternity, though as sentences are counted in trillions of years, this must be considered small comfort indeed.

In other parts of the Buddhist world Jigoku is translated as Nakara, but it is the Japanese term that has been taken up by the horror-movie industry. The 1960 movie *Jigoku* (known in English as *The Sinners of Hell*), with its Jekyll-and-Hyde central characters, is regarded as one of the most influential of the genre and has been remade several times over the decades.

Jorogumo

In Japanese mythology, this is a deadly creature that can transform itself from a spider into a beautiful woman in order to seduce and kill. In modern Japanese the name translates as "entangling bride," but this has been adapted from a less attractive earlier meaning: "whore spider." According to tradition, when a golden orb-weaver spider reaches the age of 400 years, it develops magical powers and a taste for human rather than insect prey. The resulting spider woman lures virile young men into her web with the promise of sexual favors, ensnaring them in its strong silk fibers. As she feasts on each victim, she releases a powerful venom that weakens him, enabling her to savor his lingering death.

The Jorogumo is not Japan's only shape-shifting spider. There's also the Tsuchigumo, which spins a silken web in which to trap (and subsequently eat) humans or animals much larger than itself. In another version of its legend it grows to a gigantic size, but the result is the same. The Tsuchigumo can transform itself into anything from a servant boy who administers poison to a wounded samurai under the pretext that it is medicine, to a beautiful woman leading troops into battle. It's probably wise to be wary of any spiders encountered in Japan.

Juggernaut

In modern parlance, a very large lorry, or a great force that plows ruthlessly and unhesitatingly through anything that stands in its way. But in Hinduism the word refers to something even more destructive. Juggernaut or Jagannath, meaning "lord of the world," is a title of the god Krishna, who is himself an avatar of the supreme god Vishnu. Juggernaut is worshipped in the Indian city of Puri, where a temple dating back to the twelfth century houses an image of him as an odd-looking creature with bulging eyes, a blood-red mouth, and no limbs. Every year the citizens of Puri place the image on a heavy chariot and parade it through the streets. Thousands of pilgrims crowd around and are occasionally crushed under the vehicle's wheels. In the past at least, this didn't happen only by accident. One Friar Odoric, a witness to the festival in the fourteenth century, reported that worshippers "cast themselves under the chariot, so that its wheels may go over them, saying that they desire to die for their god."

Juju

With a name taken from the Hausa language of Nigeria, this is a charm or FETISH (see page 75) with supposed magical or supernatural powers, or the power associated with such an object. One nineteenth-century traveler in West Africa reported that the guava was the "ju-ju or fetish tree of these people," while the African-American missionary Amanda Berry Smith (1837–1915), entering the home of an important chief, recorded that:

> *... the first thing we saw on entering was in one corner of the courtyard a large juju, the head of an elephant, which represents a superstition they all believe in, and which they all have, in some shape or form, in their houses. They also have the skulls of goats, numbers of human skulls, turtle shells, chicken feathers, lots of long strings, or bits of rag, hanging in strings and tied in different knots and loops, and plenty of dirty grease poured over them.*

Clearly, almost anything could serve as a juju if it was in the right place or used by the right person. The term can also mean the atmosphere of a place, and the suggestion of something feeling unlucky or just not quite right: a combination of karma and bad vibes, perhaps.

Kappa

See Vodník (page 244).

Kelpie

Often taking the form of a horse, this is a shape-shifting water spirit of Lowland Scotland who has been known to drown travelers or, more helpfully, to use its water power to keep mills going during the night. Scottish lore is well provided with such beasties: the poet Robert Burns, in a letter of 1787, recalled an old woman whom he had known in his childhood and who was "remarkable for her ignorance, credulity, and superstition":

> *She had, I suppose, the largest collection in the country of tales and songs concerning devils, ghosts, fairies, brownies, witches, warlocks, spunkies, kelpies, elf-candles, dead-lights, wraiths, apparitions, cantraips, giants, enchanted towers, dragons, and other trumpery. This cultivated the latent seeds of poetry, but had so strong an effect on my imagination, that to this hour, in my nocturnal rambles, I sometimes keep a sharp look out in suspicious places.*

He obviously never grew out of this fascination. In another letter, written five years later—and only four years before his death—he was imagining himself addressing unidentified spirits around the witching time of night (see witching hour, page 258); alongside the possibility that they might be bogles, brownies, or ghosts, he declaimed:

> *Be thou a kelpie, haunting the ford or ferry, in the starless night, mixing thy laughing yell with the howling of the storm and the roaring of the flood, as thou viewest the perils and miseries of man on the foundering horse, or in the tumbling boat!*

Kladenets

Another magical sword (see Angurvadel, page 11, and Balisarda, page 20, for more), this one features in Russian lore and has the advantage over many others of being self-swinging. It's usually to be found in the possession of a *bogatyr,* a type of elite warrior who features in many Russian folk tales. The name kladenets may derive from a Slavic word for treasure, and some stories have it lurking behind a wall or under a sacred tree, waiting for the *bogatyr* to discover it and put its magic powers to suitable use: among its many exploits, it may have been the weapon St George used to slay his legendary dragon.

Korrigan

Its name being the Breton for "small dwarf," this is a creature that can take various forms: it's often depicted as a beautiful woman with long, flowing hair who, siren-like, sings as she combs her golden tresses, luring the men she seduces to their death. She is, however, seen at her best only in dim light, which disguises her red eyes and pale, wrinkled skin.

The American anthropologist Walter Evans-Wentz (1878–1965) took a different view; he recorded korrigans as evil spirits, condemned to do penance on Earth for an unspecified time. Prone to dancing around fountains, they could be identified by a simple test: asking them to list the days of the week. The sanctity of the Sabbath meant that these wicked creatures were unable to pronounce its name.

Krampus

A famous Christmas song tells us that Santa Claus knows who has been naughty over the preceding year and who has been nice, and in much of Central Europe St Nicholas (the fourth-century bishop whose name gave rise to Santa Claus) traditionally has an alarming companion called Krampus to deal with the naughty ones. Krampus is usually depicted as a hairy demon with cloven hoofs, fangs, and a frighteningly long tongue; his role is to leave coal rather than presents for the undeserving children and even, in extreme cases, tote them away in a basket. The tradition crossed the Atlantic with the European emigrants of the nineteenth century and can still be found in U.S. Christmas celebrations, reminding children of the consequences of bad behavior.

A similar figure known as *El Hombre del Saco* (the Sack Man) features in Spanish mythology. An ugly and gaunt man, he captures naughty children in broad daylight, carries them off in his sack, and, depending on which part of the country you're in and whose stories you listen to, either eats them or sells them.

Lethean

The Styx (see STYGIAN, page 219) wasn't the only river in the Underworld as envisaged by the ancient Greeks and Romans. There was also the Lethe, the river of forgetfulness—once you crossed it or drank its waters you forgot what had happened to you in your previous life. Virgil's *Aeneid*, written between 29 and 19 BCE, suggests that this made people happier rather than otherwise:

Now, by the banks of Lethe, here below,
They lose the memory of their former state,
And from the silent waters, as they flow,
Drink the oblivious draught, and all their cares forego.

Lethean, therefore, means pertaining to or causing forgetfulness of the past, and more recent poets agree with Virgil's idea of oblivion being carefree: Edgar Allen Poe, mourning the death of the woman he loves in his poem "Ulalume" (1847), refers to "the Lethean peace of the skies," while William Cowper, in his satirical epic *The Task* (1785), tells us that a craftsman "Takes a Lethean leave of all his toil" when he is lured to the pub at the end of the working day.

Leviathan

The Old Testament Book of Isaiah describes Leviathan as "the gliding serpent ... the coiling serpent ... the monster of the sea"; the Book of Job is rather more eloquent:

> *Can you pull in Leviathan with a fishhook or tie down its tongue with a rope? Can you put a cord through its nose or pierce its jaw with a hook? Will it keep begging you for mercy? Will it speak to you with gentle words? Will it make an agreement with you for you to take it as your slave for life? Can you make a pet of it like a bird or put it on a leash for the young women in your house? ... Can you fill its hide with harpoons or its head with fishing spears?*

The answer to all these questions is clearly "no," as the text goes on:

> *If you lay a hand on it, you will remember the struggle and never do it again! Any hope of subduing it is false; the mere sight of it is overpowering. No one is fierce enough to rouse it.*

The word's derivation is uncertain, but one possibility is that it comes ultimately from an Arabic word meaning to twist; some seventeenth-century biblical commentators suggested that the monster's size indicated it was not one beast but several entwined together. This may have been in the mind of the philosopher Thomas Hobbes when he called his classic work of political philosophy *Leviathan* in 1651; certainly the subtitle—*the Matter, Form, and Power of a Commonwealth, Ecclesiastical and Civil*—suggests he knew he was dealing with something huge and complicated.

Many authors since Hobbes have used the word leviathan in that sense—to describe anything large and complex, particularly something that finds its way into areas where it may not belong. The controversial Texas congressman Ron Paul (born 1935), for example, had this to say about the way his country was run:

> *Income taxes are responsible for the transformation of the Federal government from one of limited powers into a vast leviathan whose tentacles reach into almost every aspect of American life.*

Lhiannan shee

This is the spelling you might find in the Isle of Man; there's an Irish equivalent, *leannán sídhe*, and a Scottish Gaelic one, *leannan sìth*. The name translates as "fairy lover" and, as in so many other legends throughout this book and around the world, it refers to a beautiful woman who seduces and enslaves mortal men. The unusual quality here, though, is that the lhiannan shee acts as a sort of muse, inspiring the lover to great, if short-lived, powers of creativity—according to an 1888 book of Irish folk tales edited by the poet W.B. Yeats, it "lives upon the vitals of its chosen, and they waste and die."

Lilith

She's not mentioned in the biblical Book of Genesis, but in later Jewish literature Lilith appears either as Adam's first wife, banished from the Garden of Eden before Adam and Eve's contretemps with the serpent, or as a later companion. In the latter context she is said to have given birth to Adam's demonic offspring, who are sometimes described as incubi or succubi (see INCUBUS, page 120). In Jewish folklore Lilith features as a nocturnal demon, often depicted with eagle-like talons instead of feet and believed to steal babies away from their parents at night. Derived from an earlier Mesopotamian creature, her name is usually translated as "night monster." The New American Bible of 1970 refers in the Book of Isaiah to "the Lilith," a term rendered in the seventeenth-century King James's version of the bible as "screech owl."

Limbo

In medieval Christian belief, limbo was a region on the fringes of Hell where unbaptized infants and the righteous who had lived before the time of Christ (and therefore hadn't had the opportunity to be baptized) resided. Unlike Purgatory (see page 189), there was no suffering—limbo had neither the bliss of Heaven nor the torments of Hell.

In casual modern parlance, limbo is any unpleasant state of being forgotten or stuck in a position where you can't make progress until something beyond your control is resolved. As singer/songwriter Bob Dylan put it, "Being on tour is like being in limbo. It's like going from nowhere to nowhere."

From the Latin for edge or border, the word has nothing to do with the dance that requires you to bend backward in order to get under an ever-lowering bar: that is probably connected to "limber," which means supple, flexible, easily bent.

Liminal

Limen is the Latin for a threshold, so liminal describes something that is on a threshold or boundary; in OCCULT terms (see page 176) a liminal space is something on the boundaries of this world and another, between the physical and the spiritual, the familiar and the inexplicable. Imagine an eerie movie in which a traveler on a lonely road stops at a convenience store or gas station and feels there is something peculiar about it. When they try to find it on a map, it isn't there. When they tell other people about it, they discover that there is no such building on that road. Or that there used to be, but it burned down fifty years ago. Has it appeared just for a moment, out of nowhere or out of the past, for reasons that may become clear later? This is the sort of gray area that might be described as a liminal space. The poet Eleanor Rees (born 1978), whose work has been said (by fellow poet Penelope Shuttle) to invoke "a shimmering dividing line between the living and the dead," describes liminal space as "balancing on the unseen." On a more mundane level, Elly Griffiths, in her 2025 novel *The Frozen People*, uses the word to describe the detachment a passenger so often feels on the London Underground:

> *He sits in a zombie-like daze. In this way, of course, he fits in well. It's too early for the home-going commuters and the majority of the travellers are in a liminal zone of their own, headphones on, lost in time.*

La Llorona

Spanish for "the weeping woman," this refers to a legendary woman in Spanish-American tradition whose wailing leads both adults and children to their untimely deaths. Details of the story vary, but one of the most widespread is that the woman, Maria, was either mistreated by her husband or abandoned by him. In a fit of jealous rage, she subsequently lured their two sons to the local river and drowned them, before being overcome by remorse and drowning herself. Her ghost now perpetually wanders the Earth, crying out for her lost boys.

An alternative version has Maria stealing other people's children, in mistake for her own or to replace her own. Like the Bogey-man (see page 31) and other similar figures mentioned in that entry, she is a threat parents hold over the heads of children who refuse to go to bed.

Lucifer

Literally "bearer of light," this is another name for the morning star—the planet Venus when it appears in the sky before sunrise. It's also the name of the archangel who rebelled against God and was punished by being sent to Hell, the implication being that this was a particularly bright light that had been cast into the darkness. In Shakespeare's *Henry VIII* (c. 1613), Cardinal Wolsey, facing his own disgrace, muses on the perilous position of someone who depends on a king's favor:

> *When he falls, he falls like Lucifer,*
> *Never to hope again.*

It's perhaps his brightness that has led to Lucifer becoming such a popular and charismatic figure in modern fantasy culture: the Marvel Comics character Lucifer Morningstar, inspiration for the TV series *Lucifer,* has the superpower of being able to look into someone's eyes and make them tell him their true desires. He's also sexually insatiable and apparently irresistible; able to SHAPE-SHIFT (see page 205), he has decided on his current persona of a handsome young Englishman because he finds people easier to charm in this guise. It's not strictly accurate to claim, as Lucifer Morningstar does, that he is the Devil's son, but he gets away with it, as he gets away with many things.

Lwa

A group of as many as a thousand spirits from the Caribbean VOODOO religion (see page 245), acting as intermediaries between mortals and the creator god Bondye. Like the Christian saints, each lwa or loa has its own personality and responsibilities. One of the most fearsome is Baron Samedi, mentioned under TONTON MACOUTE (see page 232); another is Baron Criminel, said to be the spirit of the first murderer to have been condemned to death, now called upon to pass swift judgment on earthly crimes. Someone possessed by the spirit of Baron Criminel becomes violent and abusive, threatening to bite chunks out of the arm of anyone who offers him food he doesn't like.

Not all lwa are unpleasant, though: there's a whole family grouping called Erzulie who can be quite sympathetic. Erzulie Dantor, for example, is a spirit of love often depicted with her infant son in images reminiscent of the Virgin Mary with the Christ Child. She is also shown with scars on her face, said to have been made as a result of her resistance to slavery; to this day she is seen as a protector of women, children, and the oppressed. As is common with lwa spirits, she may "take possession" of a human subject and speak to the mortal world through them. She imparts spiritual wisdom, in contrast with Erzulie Freda, whose remit is material wealth and comfort.

Lwa is pronounced like the French word *loi*, meaning "law," and it has been suggested that there is a connection, because of the influence of French Roman Catholic law on the culture of Haiti and other Caribbean islands where voodoo is widespread.

Lycanthropy

From Greek words meaning "wolf man," this was a condition recognized in ancient times whereby sufferers imagined themselves to be wolves and assumed wolflike characteristics, notably running wild and ravenously eating inappropriate things. The author and scholar Robert Burton wrote in his 1621 *Anatomy of Melancholy* about:

> *Lycanthropia ... or Wolf madness, when men run howling about graves and fields in the night, and will not be persuaded but that they are Wolves, or some such beasts.*

Later, in the nineteenth century, lycanthropy was recorded not as a disease but as a crime, whose perpetrators were likely to be guilty of WITCHCRAFT (see page 256) who malevolently turned themselves into wolves.

There are obvious overlaps between lycanthropes (as those afflicted by lycanthropy are called) and WEREWOLVES (see page 253), the main difference being that nobody, except perhaps the sufferers themselves, claimed that being a werewolf was a disease.

Lygophobia

This may be what Helena in *A Midsummer Night's Dream* (c. 1595) was suffering from when she begged Demetrius not to desert her (see DARKLING, page 55). From Greek, it simply means being afraid of the dark, and specifically of twilight, the time when it is not yet dark but heading that way. In Greek mythology, the Titan Astraeus is the god of twilight and is married to Eos, goddess of the dawn, so they are the deities to appease if you're worried about anything that might be happening as light turns to dark or dark turns to light.

Once twilight has passed, your fear may turn to nyctophobia or scotophobia. Again, these derive from Greek, *nycto-* meaning night and *scoto-* darkness. Like all phobias (see TAPHEPHOBIA, page 222), they are abnormal fears and involve not merely the darkness itself but whatever unseen horrors the darkness may be covering. Be careful, by the way, to spell this sort of scotophobia with a lower case s; with a capital it means an intense dislike of all things Scottish, which may not be what you intend to convey.

Maenad

Female attendants on the Greek god of wine Dionysus (see SATYR, page 198, for the male equivalent), the Maenads were said to be possessed by the god during the orgiastic rites that celebrated him; they performed frenzied dances and were strong enough to tear people apart. (They are said to have done this to the musician Orpheus, after he resisted their advances because he was mourning his lost wife, Eurydice.) Their Roman counterparts were the Bacchantes, worshippers of Bacchus and participants in bacchanals or bacchanalian orgies. "Bacchanalian" is more commonly used in modern English than "maenadic," though a 1905 edition of the *Pall Mall Gazette* did refer to:

> *... the maenadic proceedings of three or four hundred young gentlemen of Oxford and Cambridge universities ... as a sequel to the Rugby match.*

Maiden

In Wiccan tradition (see page 254), the Maiden is the first phase of the deity known as the Triple Goddess; she is followed by the Mother and the Crone or Hag (see page 101), and between them they reflect the three stages of a woman's life (birth, sexual maturity, and old age/death). But in Scotland and northern England from the sixteenth century the word had a more sinister application: in use over two centuries before the guillotine became notorious in France, between 1564 and 1716 the Maiden beheaded some 150 criminals in Edinburgh, including various members of the Scottish nobility accused of treason. Made primarily of oak but with a metal blade, it was constructed in such a way that it could be dismantled and flat-packed for storage between executions. Today it can be seen in the National Museum of Scotland, just a few minutes' walk from the Mercat Cross where it carried out its grisly work.

Like the guillotine, the Maiden did its job speedily and was therefore deemed more humane than the axe or the sword, both of which grew blunt all too easily, meaning that the executioner might need multiple blows to sever the victim's head. This association with gentleness, or the fact that it was a new and unsullied device, may explain why it was called a Maiden.

This "humane" Maiden is not to be confused with the Iron Maiden, an instrument of torture in the form of an upright box in roughly human shape, lined with iron spikes. The victim was put into the box, the door was shut, and ... you can guess the rest. This hideous device seems to have been most widespread in Germany and other parts of east-central Europe, but its history is vague: the German polymath Johann Keyssler, writing in the 1740s, describes it as an instrument "concerning which so many idle stories are told."

Makutu

The Maori word for a spell or incantation, this is a form of WITCHCRAFT (see page 256) once practiced among the Indigenous people of New Zealand, first recorded by the missionary Thomas Kendall in 1820. Largely used by the *tohunga* or priest/doctor of a community, it could cause the death of the person against whom the spell was cast—so it was particularly important that power didn't fall into the wrong hands, as the New-Zealand-born linguist Johann Baucke (1846–1931) observed in *Where the White Man Treads* in 1905:

> *And yet another decimating tool in the hands of spite and revenge was makutu (witchcraft), faith in which rested on no more solid base than fear – abject, craven fear; fear, which once it got its talons in the vitals was as certain in its action as poison! Let one fear that a makutu spell had been laid upon him, neither bravery, strength, nor health would avail to avert the decree; he would go to bed forthwith and – die! ... It was a dangerous weapon in the hands of the vindictive and unscrupulous.*

Maleficium

In the seventeenth century, "maleficium" was a legal term defined as an act of WITCHCRAFT (see page 256) intended to cause harm or injury. It comes from the Latin for an evil deed or sorcery; the perpetrator of such a deed was a malefactor, a word used in modern English to denote someone who performs any sort of criminal act, not just a SATANIC one (see page 197). The damage caused by a maleficium could be anything from hurting or bringing about the death of a victim to destroying their property or interfering with the weather with malicious intent (as, for example, conjuring up the sort of storm described under FITH-FATH, see page 76).

Mandrake

A number of solanaceous plants, of which mandrake is one, are poisonous, narcotic, or hallucinogenic, which may explain why they have often been believed to have magic powers. Mandrake's long, forked root can look disturbingly human-like, which may have added to the belief that it was an aid to fertility. It's mentioned in that context in the biblical Book of Genesis, and the sixteenth-century Italian politician Machiavelli wrote a play called *The Mandrake* in which the plant's value as an aid to conception is a driving factor in the plot.

There seems to be no scientific basis for the legend that mandrake screamed when you uprooted it and that the person doing the uprooting would die, but for a legend with no basis it is remarkably widespread. Shakespeare in particular seems to have loved it. In *King Henry VI, Part II* (1591), the Duke of Suffolk is accused of not having the spirit to curse his enemies, and he replies:

> *Would curses kill, as doth the mandrake's groan,*
> *I would invent as bitter-searching terms,*
> *As curst, as harsh, and horrible to hear...*

But curses (unlike the mandrake's groan) *don't* kill, he means, so there's no point in them. In the scene in *Romeo and Juliet* (1590s) in which Juliet prepares to take the drug that will persuade people she is dead, she imagines waking up immured in the family tomb and surrounded by her dead ancestors:

> *Alack, alack, is it not like that I,*
> *So early waking, what with loathsome smells,*
> *And shrieks like mandrakes torn out of the earth,*
> *That living mortals, hearing them, run mad.*

All that apart, the word mandrake derives from the plant's botanical name *Mandrogara,* which may go back to the Persian for "man plant." Sixteenth-century writers (including the herbalist John Gerard, see BELLADONNA, page 27) sometimes called the plant *mandragon*, which just added to the mystique.

Manticore

Mythologies the world over feature creatures that are part human, part something else, and the manticore is the Persian contribution. Its name may come from a Persian term meaning "man eater" and it is more complex than many such beasts, combining the head of a man, the body of a lion or tiger, a scorpion-like stinging tail, and sometimes quills along its back which it can use as poisoned arrows. It is also notably ferocious, with two or three sets of teeth, and is reputed to eat its victims whole, bones and all. John Skelton, poet at the court of Henry VIII, wrote a lengthy satire called (in modern spelling) *The Book of Philip Sparrow*, in which a young girl apparently mourns the death of her pet bird and rains down curses on the head of the cat that killed it:

The serpents of Libany [*Lebanon*]
Might sting thee venomously!
The dragons with their tongues
Might poison thy liver and lungs!
The manticores of the mountains
Might feed them on thy brains!

Skelton's verse is lampooning more serious elegies, but it confirms that the manticore—alongside the serpent and the dragon—as a force to be seriously reckoned with.

Medium

A go-between, an intermediary, or more specifically someone who presides at a SÉANCE (see page 202) and acts as the conduit through which the living and the dead can communicate. Like many words connected with this form of SPIRITUALISM (see page 217), it emerged in the mid-nineteenth century, when scientific research into things supernatural was first taken seriously. An American lawyer named Lucien C. Boynton, keeping a journal in 1851, reported that he had attended a séance at which "A Mr White from Providence, a mason by trade, is the 'medium.'" Boynton's use of what are called "distance quotes" indicates that the word is a new coining, or at least new to the author in this context; once this meaning of medium becomes familiar, the inverted commas disappear.

Mephistophelean

Related to *Mephistopheles*, an evil spirit in German folklore best known through the story of Faust, the scholar who sold his soul to the Devil in return for unlimited knowledge and pleasure. According to Christopher Marlowe's play *The Tragical History of Doctor Faustus,* published in about 1604, after the author's death, Mephistophilis (as he spells it) and his companion Belzebub are:

> *Unhappy spirits that fell with Lucifer,*
> *Conspir'd against our God with Lucifer,*
> *And are for ever damn'd with Lucifer.*

Mephistophilis can perform only what LUCIFER (see page 142) commands. More importantly, he will serve a mortal master for a fixed number of years, then claim their soul for Lucifer at the end.

The name probably comes from the Greek meaning "lover of the dark" (though an alternative suggestion is that it derives from Hebrew words for "destroyer" and "liar"); the adjective taken from it means fiendish, either in appearance or character—or very likely both. Herman Melville even applied it to a whale in *Moby-Dick* (1851). In his description of what he calls a Black Fish, the narrator Ishmael writes:

> *So, call him the Hyena Whale, if you please. His voracity is well known, and from the circumstance that the inner angles of his lips are curved upwards, he carries an everlasting Mephistophelean grin on his face.*

Mesmerize

Franz Mesmer (1734–1815) was a German physician who invented a therapeutic system he named after himself: Mesmerism. Although later discredited, it enjoyed a considerable vogue in both Vienna and Paris and is still regarded as the forerunner of modern medical hypnosis.

Although his method may have passed into history, Mesmer's name lives on in the word "mesmerize," meaning to fascinate, to hold spellbound, as if by hypnosis. Early uses harked back to Mesmer's scientific, or pseudoscientific, practices (mesmerists could, apparently, mesmerize water, making it particularly good at quenching the thirst), but the word had taken on its metaphorical sense by the time D.H. Lawrence published *Women in Love* in 1920. One of the women of the title, Gudrun, is visiting the family of the man with whom she will soon enter a destructive relationship. He has been wandering in and out of the room and is obviously thinking about something else, but as she is about to say her goodbyes he asks her not to leave:

> *Gudrun sat down, as if, absent as he was, his will had power over her. She felt almost mesmerised ... What was he thinking, what was he feeling, as he stood there so rapt, saying nothing? He kept her—she could feel that. He would not let her go.*

Mètminwi

Known in Haiti, where his name is a contraction of the French *Maître Minuit* or "Master Midnight," this is another BOGEY-MAN (see page 31) figure. He doesn't prey only on children, though: endowed with incredibly long legs, he prowls around after midnight and catches and eats anyone who is still out and about.

For other frightening beings from Haiti, see LWA (page 143) and TONTON MACOUTE (page 232).

Miasma

A seventeenth-century text with the extraordinary title *Medela medicinæ a plea for the free profession and renovation of the art of physick, out of the noblest and most authentick writers ... : tending to the rescue of mankind from the tyranny of diseases, and of physicians themselves* makes reference to "The Miasma or Malign Inquination [pollution] of blood and humors." So as early as this, the literal meaning of miasma—a noxious vapor rising from decaying organic matter, marshland, and the like to pollute the surrounding air—had been extended to include other evil, unpleasant, and foul-smelling influences, in this instance a form of blood poisoning.

The word comes from the Greek meaning to stain, sully, or defile, and can also be used metaphorically to convey an atmosphere of foreboding. Samuel Beckett's 1938 novel *Murphy* describes the atmosphere in Lincoln's Inn Fields, haunt of London barristers, as "foul, a miasma of laws."

Minotaur

A monster from Greek mythology, the offspring of Pasiphae, wife of King Minos of Crete, and a bull with whom she had become infatuated, thanks to a curse put upon her by the sea god Poseidon. The Minotaur (the name is a combination of Minos and the Greek for bull), being very strong and fierce, was enclosed in the world's first labyrinth—a complex maze from which it couldn't find its way out.

The city of Athens, having lost a war against Crete, was forced to send an annual tribute to Minos; it took the form of seven young men and seven young women who were then fed to the Minotaur. When the time for the third of these tributes came around, the Athenian hero Theseus vowed to put a stop to it by slaying the Minotaur; in this he was helped by one of Minos's daughters, Ariadne, who fell in love with him and provided him not only with a sword with which to defend himself against the monster, but with a ball of thread that he could use to form a trail behind him as he entered the labyrinth and thus find his way out. The plot was successful, the Minotaur was slain, and the youth of Athens saved.

That sounds like a happy ending, but there were several aftershocks. First, in his elation, Theseus forgot the promise that he had made to his father, to change his ship's black sails for white ones if his mission had prospered; as a result the old man assumed his son had been killed and threw himself from a cliff. Second, having run off with Ariadne, Theseus abandoned her on the island of Naxos. Classical sources from Homer onward give different explanations for this callous behavior, but it's an event that has since inspired numerous operas and ballets. As for the monster at the heart of the story, its legacy is to have given its name to a modern dung beetle—the minotaur beetle—which boasts three horn-like projections on its thorax, projecting above its lowered head.

Monkshood

So called because it looks like the cowl traditionally worn by monks, monkshood is a poisonous plant of the aconite family, also known as wolfsbane (see HENBANE, page 109) because it was once apparently used to kill wolves and, some say, WEREWOLVES (see page 253). This may be because Greek myth has it that the plant grew from the saliva of Cerberus, the three-headed dog who guarded the entrance to the Underworld. Modern witchcraft uses monkshood in a positive way, to produce protective energy during rituals, but earlier warriors simply took advantage of its poisonous properties and applied it to arrows and spears, making their weapons even deadlier than they might otherwise have been.

Morrigan

A SHAPE-SHIFTING (see page 205) goddess in Irish Celtic lore whose name translates as "great queen" or "phantom queen" (the first part of the word may be connected to *mare* as in NIGHTMARE, see page 172). Responsible for fertility but also for war and death, at SAMHAIN (see page 196) she is said to mate with the chief of the gods, known as the Dagda, to ensure that the land remains productive. Taking the form of a crow, she predicts doom and death but can also help assure victory in battle. Her connection with death means that some versions of Irish folklore link her to the BANSHEE (see page 22).

Mulligrubs

A fit of bad temper or melancholy, or an attack of stomach ache and/or diarrhea. A British dialect word dating back to the sixteenth century, included here because of the rather unpleasant suggestion in its etymology that grubs are eating away at your insides.

Mumbo-jumbo

Derived in the eighteenth century from the name of a West African god, mumbo-jumbo means not just nonsense, but that special sort of nonsense that is surrounded by ritual or high-flown language intended to impress. The term is a real put-down, as Louisa May Alcott, author of *Little Women*, showed when she was traveling in France in 1870 and wrote home to her mother: "We ... went to vespers in the old church, where we saw a good deal of mumbo-jumbo by red, purple, and yellow priests."

"Mumbo-jumbo" probably comes originally from the Mandinka language, spoken in Senegal, The Gambia, and other far-western parts of Africa; this makes it unlikely that it is connected with Jumbo, the captive elephant who, in the nineteenth century, was displayed in Paris's Jardin des Plantes and in London Zoo before being sold to the circus impresario P.T. Barnum and sent to the United States. Jumbo was born in Sudan, so it's more likely that his name came from Swahili, which is widely spoken in East Africa and contains the words *jumbe*, meaning "chief," and *jambo*, meaning "hello." It's from Jumbo the elephant that we get all the senses of the word—from jumbo shrimps to the jumbo jet—that imply great size.

Murder

There are many strange, even fanciful, collective nouns in English: why a parliament of owls? A business of ferrets? A sounder of swine? But perhaps the most macabre is murder, found in various spellings as far back as the fifteenth century to describe a gathering of crows. It is probable that the derivation is the same as for the more familiar sense of the word, an unlawful killing, perhaps because crows are traditionally associated with violent death, or because the bird's raucous cry sounds a bit like that of a murder victim. Crows are, of course, black, the color of mourning in the West; they are also scavengers, feeding on the flesh of dead animals, and therefore likely to be seen in large numbers near rotting corpses. And there's no denying that their call is on the harsh side.

A collection of the closely related raven is known as an unkindness, a term also found in the fifteenth century and ascribed to the bird's alleged neglect of its offspring. Again, its carrion-feeding habits give it a bad reputation. Danish folklore tells of a supernatural raven called a *valravn* that gained its superpowers by eating the bodies of kings who had been slain in battle and left unburied. Various versions of the story relate that the *valravn* became capable of human thought, that it could bring only bad luck, and that its curse could be undone only by drinking a boy's blood.

If that weren't enough to seal the raven's place in the annals of infamy, Shakespeare's arch-villainess Lady Macbeth invokes it when she hears that the king (who she has decided must be disposed of) is about to visit her:

> *The raven himself is hoarse*
> *That croaks the fatal entrance of Duncan*
> *Under my battlements.*

Thus, she takes us from one form of murder—or unkindness—to another.

N

Nahuelito

Loch Ness in Scotland isn't the only lake in the world reputed to be the home of an unseen monster. In Nahuel Huapi Lake in Patagonia lives Nahuelito ("Little Nahuel"), a serpent-like creature whose giant hump has sometimes —allegedly—been photographed. The name comes from the Indigenous Mapuche language and means "puma," because of the big cat that was once abundant in the area.

Namahage

The Oga peninsula is part of the Japanese island of Honshu, some 372 miles (600km) north of Tokyo. It's here that the annual Namahage Festival is held around New Year, and it's a time when children who have misbehaved during the course of the year need to be on their guard (see KRAMPUS, page 133, and TONTON MACOUTE, page 232, for two further examples of this). The Namahage are demons or ogres dressed in fearsome masks and straw capes; they go from door to door in groups of two or three and, although they will carry off children who are insolent or simply cry too much, their particular bugbear is laziness. The name comes from a local dialect way of asking, "Blisters healed yet?"—an insult aimed at those who sit cozily by the fire all day instead of helping with the chores.

Necromancy

The etymology of this word is confused, because while the ending, as in BELOMANCY (see page 28), is to do with magic or divination, the first half is a mixture of the Greek *nekros*, a corpse, and the Latin *niger*, meaning "black." So necromancy can be the art of conjuring up the dead, particularly to learn about the future from them, or it can be a more generic form of "black" magic or sorcery.

As early as the second century CE, the Roman writer Apuleius, in his fictional account of witchcraft, *The Golden Ass,* gave an example of necromancy, in the "conjuring the dead" sense. He told a story of a widow accused of having poisoned her husband in order to cover up her infidelity and inherit his property. After a priest has performed various rituals, "behold incontinently the dead body began to receive spirit, his principal veins did move, his life came again." The corpse protests at being brought back to life, but eventually confirms: "Verily I was poisoned by the meanes of my wicked wife, and so thereby yielded my bed unto an adulterer." Public opinion is now divided: should the errant wife be buried alive alongside her late husband, or would it be foolish to believe the testimony of a dead body? It's a question that the text, frustratingly, doesn't answer, although the fact that the corpse keeps talking and provides more and more evidence of the wife's misdeeds suggests that things are looking bad for her.

Supposed witches continued to evoke either the spirit or the body, in whole or in part, of a dead person throughout the following centuries, until the Witchcraft Act of 1604 specifically made it an offence to "take up any dead man, woman, or child, out of his, her, or their grave, or any other place where the dead body resteth; or the skin, bone, or any other part of any dead person, to be imployed, or used in any manner of Witchcraft, Sorcery, Charme, or Inchantment." The concept persisted, however: Bram Stoker's *Dracula* (1897) gives this description of a VAMPIRE (see page 243):

> *... so strong in person as twenty men; he is of cunning more than mortal, for his cunning be the growth of ages; he have still the aids of necromancy ... and all the dead that he can come nigh to are for him at command.*

Necropolis

Like NECROMANCY (see page 167), this is connected with death; the second part of the word comes from the Greek for city, as in metropolis. Thus a necropolis is a city of the dead—a burial site or cemetery, especially a large one with elaborate tombs. The word can have a metaphorical sense, too: Lafcadio Hearn, a Greek-born scholar with an interest in all things Japanese, wrote in 1895 about the prospect of some Japanese statues ending up in the British Museum: "I fancied them immured somewhere in that vast necropolis of dead gods." Thirty years earlier the French novelist Gustave Flaubert had been even more imaginative. In a letter of 1866 to his fellow novelist George Sand, commiserating with her on the death of a friend, he remarked: "That loss is added to others. How we keep these dead souls in our hearts. Each one of us carries within himself his necropolis."

Nefarious

Meaning wicked, sinful, villainous, from the Latin for "against divine law," nefarious began life as a decidedly serious word. "Bloody men," the sixteenth-century author William Painter warned, "commonly be most willingly disposed after a good time to commit some nefarious deed."

As time went on, though, it became permissible to use it with tongue in cheek. In *Our Mutual Friend* (1864–5), Charles Dickens explains how the social-climbing Mr Veneering goes about reinventing himself by casting off old acquaintances and making new ones:

> *Twemlow had first known Veneering at his club, where Veneering then knew nobody but the man who made them known to one another, who seemed to be the most intimate friend he had in the world, and whom he had known two days—the bond of union between their souls, the nefarious conduct of the committee respecting the cookery of a fillet of veal, having been accidentally cemented at that date.*

Was the veal too rare or too well done? Too hot or too cold? It's never mentioned again, so we are left to decide for ourselves, but clearly the committee had failed badly—nay, nefariously—in its duty.

Nemesis

In Greek mythology, the goddess of retribution; a personification of the gods' resentment of—and subsequent punishment of—a lack of respect towards themselves. Acts of what the Greeks called *hubris*, the pride that came before a fall, were punished by Nemesis. In modern parlance, nemesis (no longer a proper name) can be any form of retribution, or an inevitable price to be paid for a misdeed; more casually it is a hurdle that can't be overcome, a stumbling block or Waterloo; or an archenemy who can't be defeated. Superman and Sherlock Holmes are just two fictional characters who are beset by their personal nemeses, Lex Luthor, and Moriarty respectively.

Niflheim

Another version of Hell, this time in Norse mythology. Under the rule of the goddess Hel, Niflheim is a cold, dark, and misty realm to which the souls of the wicked are condemned. It's an Icelandic word, meaning "dark world," the first part probably related to ***nebula***.

Niflheim isn't often used outside this context, but in Thomas Hardy's novel *The Woodlanders* (1887) it becomes a metaphor for misunderstanding and lost love. Giles, a woodsman, is working high up in a tree on a foggy day, when Grace, on the ground below, comes to tell him that her father has promised her to another man. Giles says nothing, but remains in his tree, hidden by the fog. If, instead, he had come down and begged Grace to marry him, she thinks she might have defied her father and accepted him:

> *But he continued motionless and silent in that gloomy Niflheim or fog-land which involved him, and she proceeded on her way.*

Nightmare

Etymologically there may be some overlap or confusion with "mare," meaning a female horse, but the *-mare* part of nightmare comes from a different source, an Old English word for a spirit believed to make a sleeping person feel as if they were suffocating. From that it developed to mean the feeling of suffocation itself, and from there the current sense of any frightening dream. The slightly tautological "nightmare" dates from about 1300 for the spirit; the sixteenth century for the feeling of strangulation (always called "the nightmare"); and the nineteenth century for the modern sense, without the definite article. Most people would describe any bad dream as a nightmare, but a 1909 edition of the London-based *Daily Chronicle* newspaper made an interesting distinction:

> *Nightmare, properly so-called, is ... the further insanity of dreamland ... A healthy bad dream, however intolerable, is a normal act of the sleeping mind; a nightmare is abnormal.*

More recently, "nightmare" has been dumbed down to mean any unpleasant experience, whether waking or sleeping: noisy neighbors, getting across town during the rush hour, or working towards a tight deadline can all be described as a nightmare. Gerald Ford, being sworn in as President of the United States in 1974, after the resignation of Richard Nixon in the wake of the Watergate scandal, used it slightly more seriously:

> *Our long national nightmare is over. Our Constitution works; our great Republic is a Government of laws and not of men.*

Even so, he clearly meant that you could have a nightmare when you were wide awake.

Nisse

Also spelled *nis,* this is a word of Scandinavian origin, related to the folklore of that region. A nisse is a friendly, benevolent goblin—benevolent, that is, as long as you feed it porridge once a year, around the time of the Winter Solstice, which falls just days before Christmas in the northern hemisphere. This seasonal pattern has led to the nisse being associated with Santa Claus and his elves, an association made stronger by the fact that he is generally depicted wearing a red, pointed hat.

According to the Danish author Hans Christian Andersen, the nisse's gastronomic treat doesn't have to be porridge: in his 1852 story "The Nisse and the Huckster," the nisse chooses to live with the huckster "because at Christmas he always had a large dish full of jam, with a great piece of butter in the middle." However, the nisse is strongly attracted to the huckster's lodger, a student who reads from a book of poetry that delights him. Indeed, when the house is threatened by fire, the nisse saves the book as being "the greatest treasure in the house." So strong are his feelings that he is tempted to leave the huckster altogether and move in with the student; but once the panic of the fire has subsided, he thinks again. "I must divide myself between the two," he decides at last; "I cannot quite give up the huckster, because of the jam."

Obi

Not to be confused with the Japanese sash of the same name, this is an amulet or charm used in WITCHCRAFT (see page 256) in the Caribbean and can also denote the witchcraft itself. Sometimes spelled *obeah*, it's a word of West African origin and crossed the Atlantic with the enslaved people from that part of the world in the seventeenth century or so. One eighteenth-century British traveler, who visited a number of islands in the Caribbean, observed that "Old Nails, Glass, Stones, Rags, &c ... being put together and tied in a Rag ... is called the *Obeah*," while another, writing specifically about Jamaica, recorded:

> *They sometimes do much mischief by administering poisons, of which they have various kinds in the island, some of them very subtile and lingering in their effects. The general name ... for these poisons is obea.*

Occult

From the Latin for hidden, this word usually carries an additional sense of the supernatural: it means beyond normal human understanding, magical, mystical, and potentially frightening. It can be a noun—as in the occult—or an adjective—occult practices. The sixteenth-century German philosopher Heinrich Cornelius Agrippa wrote a study called *Three Books of Occult Philosophy,* which considered the relationship between magic and religion: an eighteenth-century commentator observed that Agrippa had had "a taste for the occult sciences, alchemy, divination, dæmonurgy, and astrology."

Away from the context of magic, occult—like ARCANE (see page 14) and ESOTERIC (see page 70)—suggests something that is understandable only to the initiated, the chosen few: in 1841 the essayist Isaac d'Israeli was writing about printing as "a secret and occult art," and a generation later Karl Marx said of financial capital that it had "acquired the occult ability to add value to itself. It brings forth living offspring, or, at the least, lays golden eggs."

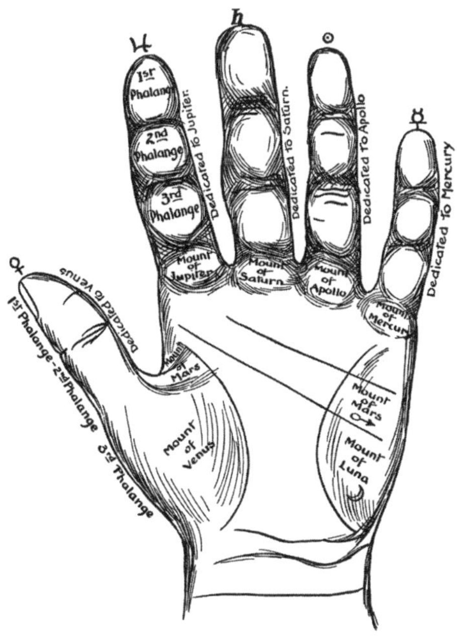

Ordeal

A common enough word in modern English, meaning any particularly difficult experience that tests one's character or endurance, or is just long-lasting and painful. This had a more SINISTER (see page 208) meaning in the days when supposed WITCHCRAFT (see page 256) was rife and witches were much persecuted. Ordeal by water—also known as "swimming"—saw the suspected witch tied up, then thrown into the local pond or lake while still attached to a rope, so that they could be pulled out when the test was over, alive or dead. If the accused drowned, they were declared innocent; if they floated, they were deemed guilty of witchcraft, hauled out, tried, convicted, and usually hanged. The rationale behind this form of judgment was that water—being the medium of baptism in the Christian church and therefore having some innate sense of good and evil—would reject a witch.

Other ordeals, not necessarily as a test of witchcraft, involved plunging the accused's hand into boiling water (quick healing was a sign of God's intercession and therefore the accused's innocence); or the so-called "ordeal of the bier," when a suspected murderer was made to approach or touch the corpse of their supposed victim, and was found guilty if blood flowed from it.

The word "ordeal" derives from various northern European words for judgment or decision; the later meaning of a severe test, generally a long and unpleasant one, comes from the various harsh judgments just described.

Oubliette

Oublier is the French word for "to forget," and an oubliette is perhaps the most frightening kind of dungeon of all: one where they (whoever "they" are) throw you in and forget all about you. It's designed so that the only entrance is through the top; your captors can then lower food down to you on a rope and take your waste out the same way—but something in the name of the place suggests that they probably won't bother.

Adopted from French, oubliette was known in English by the eighteenth century. Alfred, Lord Tennyson (1809–92), gives this graphic description in his 1876 drama *Harold*, whose title character is the Harold who was killed at the Battle of Hastings:

> *And deeper still the deep-down oubliette,*
> *Down thirty feet below the smiling day—*
> *In blackness—dogs' food thrown upon thy head.*
> *And over thee the suns arise and set,*
> *And the lark sings, the sweet stars come and go,*
> *And men are at their markets, in their fields,*
> *And woo their loves and have forgotten thee;*
> *And thou art upright in thy living grave ...*

The lines are spoken to Harold—currently king of England—by his younger brother, who is frightened of what the invading William of Normandy will do to him if he doesn't abdicate quietly. Clearly Harold decided that being shot by an arrow in the eye was a more attractive fate than languishing in an oubliette.

Ouija

Oui and *ja* are the words for yes in French and German, respectively, but it's by no means certain that these are the origin of "ouija," which could, according to the *Oxford English Dictionary*, equally possibly come from a supposed ancient Egyptian word for good luck, or from the name of a city in Morocco. Whatever the word's origins may be, a Ouija board is a flat surface with letters, numbers, and sometimes other symbols in a circle round its perimeter; participants in a SÉANCE (see page 202) sit around it, each with a finger on an upturned glass or some sort of pointer. The MEDIUM (see page 153) in charge of the séance summons up a spirit from beyond the grave and it—or other spirits that it is able to talk to—moves the pointer from letter to letter in order to spell out answers to the questions it is asked.

Although séances and other supposed ways of contacting the dead have existed since time immemorial, the Ouija board itself was first manufactured in Baltimore in 1890 and patented a year later. It became particularly popular after the First World War, when almost everybody would have had a recently deceased loved one they might wish to contact, but it had caught the public imagination before that. In 1913 one Pearl Curran of Chicago apparently made contact with a long-dead English writer named Patience Worth and over the following years published several volumes of her work, claiming that she (Pearl) was channeling the author's words. It's very unlikely that this was true (one of the books was set in the nineteenth century, two hundred years after Patience was said to have lived), but it generated a great deal of interest in the Ouija board.

Not everyone recommends this way of contacting spirits: in the video game *Phasmophobia*, the Ouija board is one of the "cursed items" that allow players to interact directly with the GHOST (see page 84) that haunts the site of the game, but this interaction happens at the expense of their sanity.

Paranormal

The "para" part of this word means "existing alongside" or "existing beyond," so paranormal is "alongside or beyond the normal": it's used as both an adjective and a noun to designate the apparent presence of POLTERGEISTS (see page 186) , TELEKINESIS (see page 228), and other such phenomena that can't be explained by logic or by normal scientific laws. It also extends into a vast genre of books and movies, from the *Twilight* series, in which someone who seems to all intents and purposes to be a teenage boy turns out to be a 108-year-old vampire, to the *Paranormal Activity* franchise, which features an evil demon who terrorizes the inhabitants of various California houses. Communicating with the spirits of the dead, UFOs (see UFOLOGY, page 238), spontaneous combustion, and sightings of abnormally large cats outside their normal territory—all of these and more come under the heading of "the paranormal."

The same etymology also gives us "parapsychology," the study of paranormal phenomena in psychology.

Pentacle

See PENTAGRAM (page 182).

Pentagram

With *penta-* coming from the Greek for five and *-gram* from the Greek for written, this is a five-pointed, star-shaped device used for warding off evil and, in modern WICCA (see page 254), as a magic symbol for such rituals as invoking the Goddess. The word has been in use only since the nineteenth century; pentacle—literarily "a little five-sided object"—is three hundred years older and today is distinguished from a pentagram in that the pentacle's star is usually enclosed within a circle. An article in an 1833 edition of the literary *Fraser's Magazine*, discussing a new translation of Goethe's *Faust* (see MEPHISTOPHELEAN, page 154), describes an early scene in the play in which Mephistopheles follows Faust home in the guise of a poodle (a hunting dog, in those days) and then reveals his identity. Following some conversation:

> *The fiend is now at liberty to depart, but is prevented by the pentagram in the threshold from availing himself of that privilege, which pentagram as a poodle he remarked not when he entered; and it is a law binding on devils and phantoms, that they must go out the same way that they stole in ...*

As the same author goes on to explain:

> *The pentagram was ... supposed to possess the same kind of power which, amongst us, used popularly to be attributed to the horse-shoe.*

That resemblance has carried over into modern thinking: as with a horseshoe, the position of the star is significant: if it points upward it is a symbol of life; pointing downward can mean death, or can force a subject to look deeply (and probably uncomfortably) into their inner self.

Phantasmagoria

An announcement in *The Times* of October 5, 1801 informed readers:

> *... that the Phantasmagoria, or the Grand Cabinet of Optical and Mechanical Curiosities, exhibiting Magical Illusions, and various other wonderful Pieces of Art, will open ... This Day.*

The exhibition was held at London's Lyceum Theatre and consisted of various images of GHOSTS (see page 84), skeletons, and the like, projected via what was then the state-of-the-art technology known as a magic lantern. Enthusiastic spectators were encouraged to believe that they really were witnessing SPECTERS (see page 216) being brought back to life.

The concept was patented in London by a German-born magician known as Phylidor, but a *phantasmagorie* had appeared in France some years earlier, and the name had been coined there. It's taken from the Greek for a ghost or apparition (still found in English as "phantasme" or phantom) and possibly the suffix *agora* meaning a meeting place, though it's equally possible that the French creator of the *phantasmagorie* simply wanted an exotic-sounding name.

Over the years the word came to be used more loosely, to describe a shifting and extraordinary scene of dreamlike images, some of them opium-induced. But as recently as 1992 *National Geographic Traveler* used it in a more down-to-earth way to describe the "world-class" Botanical Garden in St Louis, Missouri, as "a 79-acre multifloral phantasmagoria in the center of the city."

Phantom

Originally an Anglo-Norman and Old French word whose origins (like those of PHANTASMAGORIA, see page 183) can be traced back to the Greek for "appearance," the word "phantom" has been found in English since the fourteenth century. It means much the same as GHOST (see page 84)—an insubstantial figure, usually in human form, but having no solid, physical existence. The most famous phantom is probably the one who haunts the Paris Opera House and has featured in numerous movies and musicals since Gaston Leroux's novel *The Phantom of the Opera* first appeared in 1910: this phantom is heard before he is seen, using his powers to make a renowned soprano croak like a toad and crying out in an "impossible ... mouthless voice" that her dreadful singing will bring the chandelier crashing down. As indeed it does.

Some phantoms are less destructive, though they can be distressing: a phantom pregnancy shows all the signs of pregnancy but turns out to be imaginary, while someone who has had an arm or a leg amputated may feel the sensation of a phantom limb, sometimes painful, sometimes annoyingly itchy and, of course, unable to be scratched.

Poker

Nothing to do with the card game or the implement used for poking a fire, in the world of NIGHTMARES (see page 172) a poker is anything UNCANNY (see page 240) and frightening. The term originates in Scandinavia (*pokker* in Danish; *pocker* in Swedish) and was first found in English around 1600. In the seventeenth century Tom Poker was one of many names for the scary being invoked to frighten badly behaved children: by the eighteenth Old Poker was a term for the Devil, on a par with Old Harry or Old Nick; and in 1828 the great American lexicographer Noah Webster defined poker as "any frightful object, especially in the dark."

Poltergeist

From the German for "noisy ghost," this has been a word in English since the nineteenth century and means precisely what it says it means—but not only that. Those who believe they have been haunted by a poltergeist speak of feeling extreme cold or, occasionally, extreme heat. The so-called Enfield Poltergeist, apparently heard in a house in that north London suburb in 1977, not only whistled but caused the eleven-year-old daughter of the house to talk in an old man's voice. In 1989, at what became known as Witch Farm near Brecon in Wales, the new residents of an old farmhouse experienced the smell of sulfur and incense, heard doors slamming and footsteps running up and down the stairs—and found that their electricity meter had spun out of control, landing them with an enormous bill at the end of their first winter.

So, a noisy ghost, yes, but also an alarming and malevolent one.

For more about some frightening aspects of sulfur, see BRIMSTONE (see page 36).

Poludnitsa

While most spirits, from HAGS (see page 101) to VAMPIRES (see page 243), shun the light of day and are at their most active around midnight, the Slavic Poludnitsa—known in English as "Lady Midday" or "the noon witch"—appears at that hour, as a warning against going out in the fields when the sun is at its strongest. As is often the case with folkloric characters, descriptions of her vary: she may be a beautiful young woman, dressed in white, or an old and ugly one. Either way, she tends to carry a sickle or scythe, symbolizing both her connection with agriculture and her threat to cut lives short. Those who meet her are prone to sudden illness or madness—in some stories she asks anyone she encounters difficult questions and chops off their head if they fail to answer correctly.

Poludnitsa can also be used to frighten children: in another version of the legend (which inspired an 1896 symphonic poem by Antonin Dvorak, "Polednice" or "The Noonday Witch"), a mother tells her son that, if he doesn't behave, she will call on Polednice to take him away. The boy takes no notice and, on the stroke of noon, the witch appears ...

Psychic

From the Greek meaning "of the soul of life," this adjective describes something that is outside or apparently outside the possibilities defined by natural laws, or a person who is sensitive to such things and can perhaps interpret or manipulate them. As a noun, it can also designate a person who is psychic.

The concept can be taken seriously, as in the second-century Buddhist text *Flower Garland Sutra*, which tells us that:

> *Universally Good is present in all lands*
> *Sitting on a jewelled lotus throne, beheld by all;*
> *He manifests all psychic powers*
> *And is able to enter infinite meditations.*

Alternatively, it can be scoffed at, as when Aldous Huxley wrote in 1941, with reference to the seventeenth-century French priest François du Tremblay:

> *He was deeply impressed by any manifestation of the siddhis, as the Indians call them, the psychic powers which may be aroused by meditation and to which the wiser mystics pay as little attention as possible.*

Purgatory

In Christian belief, this is the place that temporarily accommodates the souls of those who die in a state of grace; they remain there until their sins are purged—cleansed away—and they can enter the Kingdom of Heaven. *Purgatory* is the second of the three books of Dante's *Divine Comedy* (see INFERNO, page 122); in it the poet visits the Mountain of Purgatory, whose seven terraces correspond to the seven deadly sins. There he meets, among others, Adrian V, who had been pope when Dante was a boy and is expiating the sin of avarice; and a rival poet, Bonagiunta Orbicciani, in the region inhabited by the gluttonous.

Today, purgatory (with or without the initial capital) can be used loosely to mean any unpleasant situation that, unlike Hell, will come to an end sooner or later: Abraham Lincoln, who was married to the same woman for twenty-two years, is said to have observed that marriage "is neither Heaven nor Hell, it is simply Purgatory."

Rauðskinna

A legendary Icelandic GRIMOIRE (see page 94), whose name translates as "Book of Power," *Rauðskinna* has been described as a bible for all magicians, giving them the power to overcome Satan himself. It is said to have been written by a sixteenth-century bishop known as Gottskálk the Cruel (or possibly stolen by him from its true author) and buried with him. The esteemed sorcerer Galdra-Loftur, who lived some two hundred years after Gottskálk, is said to have been so determined to find Rauðskinna that his failure drove him mad; he rowed himself out to sea and disappeared, presumably drowning himself in despair.

Rawhead

Another of the many bugbears invoked to frighten children, Rawhead was in the sixteenth century frequently mentioned in the same breath as HOBGOBLINS (see page 112), WEREWOLVES (see page 253), HELLHOUNDS (see page 107), and HECATE (see page 104). He became even more terrifying when you thought about the meaning of his name: his head was literally raw, stripped of its flesh. He also frequently had a companion, the pair being known as Rawhead-and-Bloody-Bones. A sixteenth-century text with the title (in modern spelling) of *The Will of the Devil with his ten detestable commandments* refers to "Our faithful Secretaries, Hobgoblin, and Bloodybone," while the *Oxford English Dictionary* reports that Bloody Bones has been variously said "to lurk in ponds waiting to drown children" and to be "associated with the apparition of a murdered man supposed to haunt the scene of his murder."

Redman

A solitary elf of the English Midlands, known for wearing a red cap and living in wells or hollows. Like the Irish leprechaun, he can be forced to give gold to anyone who catches him. In fact, there is an Irish equivalent, *fear dearg* or *far darrig* (literally "red man"), who dresses all in red and indulges in a variety of practical jokes, the scarier, the better—he can alter his voice so that he sounds like waves crashing against rocks, or like a dull, hollow call from beyond the grave. He has been known to lure mortals into his hut and force them to make dinner from a hag skewered on a spit, and is also prone to stealing babies and leaving CHANGELINGS (see page 44) in their place.

According to folklorist Miland Brown, a similar though gorier idea is found in the Scottish Borders region, where the headgear of the redcap goblin is dipped in fresh blood—and must continue to be replenished, or the goblin will die. Like the Irish red man, he has a haunting laugh that can echo through the night; he also wears iron boots which clank threateningly as he approaches you.

Unconnectedly, "red man" was once a term used in ALCHEMY (see page 10) to signify sulfur, paired in many recipes with "white woman," meaning quicksilver or mercury. A fifteenth-century *Compound of Alchemy* tells us that "They talke of the red man & his whit wiffe."

Rusalka

See VODNÍK (page 244).

Sabbat

Etymologically related to the Christian and Jewish Sabbath and Shabbat, meaning the weekly day of rest that is traditionally devoted to religious observance, Sabbat was in the sixteenth century a time when witches and other supernatural beings met, usually at midnight and for demonic purposes (see WITCHING HOUR, page 258). In addition to this literal sense, it could be used figuratively to denote a miscellany of all things evil or eerie. The American folklorist Charles Godfrey Leland described in his 1893 memoirs a collection of stories he discovered as a boy:

> *Singly, they were appalling enough to any one in those days when the supernatural still thrilled the strongest minds, but taken altogether for steady reading, the book was a perfect Sabbat of deviltry and dramatic horrors.*

More recently, Sabbat has lost its SATANIC (see page 197) connection and become the name given in Pagan religions to the various festivals held at the equinoxes, solstices, and the so-called cross-quarter days that fall between these dates, meaning that there are eight Sabbats in a year. Two of the four major ones are Imbolc, between January 31 and February 1, which celebrates the transition from winter to spring and is marked by the lighting of fires to symbolize the returning warmth; and Lughnasa, celebrated on August 1 to mark the gathering of the harvest. For the other two, see SAMHAIN (see page 196) and WALPURGISNACHT (see page 248).

Samhain

One of the principal SABBATS (see page 195) in the Pagan calendar, the equivalent of the Christian (and secular) HALLOWE'EN (see page 102). Celebrated on the night of October 31 and November 1, it marked the start of the New Year in ancient Celtic times and was an occasion for the lighting of bonfires, whose heat was said to give strength to the sun to keep it going through the winter.

Samhain is an Irish word whose origins are disputed: it might mean "summer's end," but it has also been suggested that it means "a gathering of the living and the dead"—which would tie in with All Souls' Day (see HALLOWE'EN) and the Mexican Day of the Dead (see CALACA, page 40), both celebrated on or around November 2. Samhain is also regarded as a time of "thinning of the veil," when the barrier between this world and the next, the spiritual and the physical, is at its weakest, making it easier to communicate with ancestors and other spirits.

Sasquatch

See YETI (page 263).

Satanic

Pertaining to Satan or the Devil; hence, supremely evil. The name Satan comes from a Hebrew word meaning to plot against, so the key aspects of Satan are that he is the principal adversary of God, and that he tempts humankind into sin. William Blake's famous "dark satanic mills" (in the hymn usually known as "Jerusalem," published around 1808) have been the subject of much debate: are they literally the industrial mills that are ruining the natural landscape that Blake loved, or do they symbolize the Establishment—the Church, the universities of Oxford and Cambridge, and other such bodies of which he disapproved? It's unclear. What is clear is that he regarded them as deeply, supremely evil.

Satyr

In Greek mythology, an attendant on Dionysus, god of wine, usually represented as having a human body but the legs of a goat and short horns on the head. Satyrs were spirits of the fields and woods, particularly concerned with the fertility of these areas. Combine this interest in fertility and Dionysus's enthusiasm for wine and you have a passion for revelry in all its forms. A satyr therefore came to mean a lecher, a sexually rampant male, and satyriasis emerged as a neurotic condition, a compulsion to have sex with as many partners as possible, the equivalent of nymphomania in women. By the eighteenth century and ever since, writers had generally forgotten the Satyrs' original connection with nature and were concentrating on their sexual aspects, as in William Somerset Maugham's 1919 novel *The Moon and Sixpence*:

> *I wish I knew how to describe his smile ... it lit up his face, changing the expression, which was generally sombre, and gave it a look of not ill-natured malice. It was a slow smile, starting and sometimes ending in the eyes; it was very sensual, neither cruel nor kindly, but suggested rather the inhuman glee of the satyr.*

Scavenger's daughter

With many instruments of torture, it's easy to guess how they might have been used: victims were laid out on a rack, for example, and their limbs stretched until they were in such pain that they would confess to absolutely anything. Manacles at a certain height above the ground held the victim's wrists so that he was suspended with his arms above his head and again suffered excruciating pain.

The scavenger's daughter is less obvious: there are two versions in the Tower of London, in one of which the victim would be kneeling, in the other handcuffed not only by the wrists but also by the neck and ankles. In both, the body was compressed or contorted rather than stretched, but the excruciating pain was much the same. The name has nothing to do with scavenging—the device is said to have been invented by one Leonard Skevington, who was Lieutenant of the Tower during the reign of Henry VIII. It's worth noting, though, that, as with the Iron Maiden (see MAIDEN, page 148), women somehow get the blame.

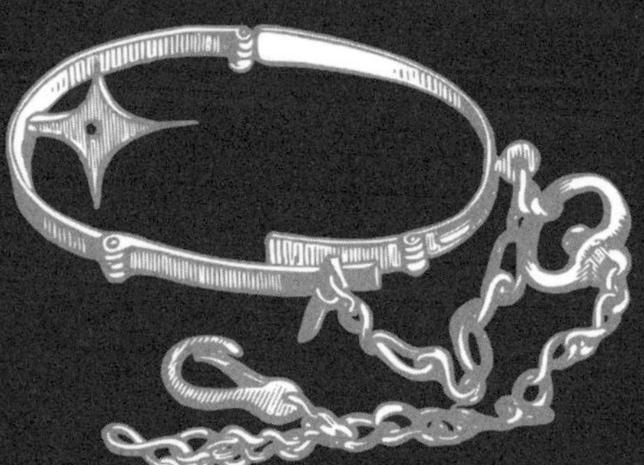

Scrying

A form of divination using a crystal ball, a mirror, or the surface of water—anything in which reflections may be seen and images of the future perceived or imagined. The practice of scrying was at its height in Elizabethan times, when the mathematician, astrologist, and occultist John Dee occupied an influential position as advisor to the Queen. In papers published after his death (in 1608 or 1609) as *A True and Faithful Relation of What passed for Many Years between Dr. John Dee and Some Spirits,* Dee writes of presenting his eldest son "to the service of Seeing and Skrying from God," and refers to his assistant or partner Edward Kelly as his "Seer, or Skryer." The word is connected to "descry," used in non-magical circles to mean to discern or discover by looking closely.

Scylla and Charybdis

In Classical mythology, the sea god Glaucus fell in love with a beautiful water nymph named Scylla, who rejected him. He sought the help of the enchantress Circe, but unfortunately, she was in love with Glaucus herself and vented her jealous rage on Scylla, turning her into a vengeful sea monster who devoured passing mariners. Scylla was positioned on one side of the narrow Strait of Messina, between Sicily and Italy; on the other side was a whirlpool named Charybdis, whose surging waters were so powerful that any vessel coming near them when the tide was rushing in was inevitably engulfed. Not even Neptune, king of the sea gods, was strong enough to control it.

Thus, any vessel that survived the onslaught of Scylla was likely to fall into the hands of Charybdis, and vice versa: the expression "between Scylla and Charybdis" came to be synonymous with "between the devil and the deep blue sea" or, more prosaically, "between a rock and a hard place." They all mean that there is little chance of escaping the situation, and that any choice you make is likely to be a bad one. As the philosopher Francis Bacon—a great believer in finding a sensible middle ground—wrote in a 1597 essay:

> *In matters of the understanding, it requires great skill and a particular felicity to steer clear of Scylla and Charybdis. If the ship strikes upon Scylla, it is dashed in pieces against the rocks; if upon Charybdis, it is swallowed outright. This allegory is pregnant with matter; but we shall only observe the force of it lies here, that a mean be observed in every doctrine and science, and in the rules and axioms thereof, between the rocks of distinctions and the whirlpools of universalities: for these two are the bane and shipwreck of fine geniuses and arts.*

Séance

The French word for sitting (hence the accent, which not everyone insists on), this is a meeting that attempts to contact the spirits of the dead. Members of a group sit in a circle and hold hands, usually in the dark or in dim light, as this is said to make it easier to communicate. A séance is conducted by a MEDIUM (see page 153), who often goes into a trance and usually operates through a "control," a spirit who conveys messages to or from the others in the room.

Sarah Penner's 2023 novel *The London Séance Society* opens with a scene, set in a French château that hasn't been lived in for a hundred years, that exactly captures the mood:

> *The clock read thirty-two minutes after midnight. Lenna Wickes, spiritualist understudy, sat at an oval table draped in black linen. A gentleman and his wife, the other séance participants, sat at the table with her. Their faces were sombre and their breathing uneasy ... Behind Lenna, blood-coloured paper peeled from the walls, clusters of mildew hiding underneath.*
>
> *If all went well tonight, the ghost they sought—that of a young woman, murdered here in this very place—would soon appear.*

Sepulchral

From the Latin for "to bury," sepulchral means pertaining to a sepulchre, a grand tomb, the sort of place where, if you were to speak above a whisper, you'd hear your voice echoing back at you. Byron (never the most understated of poets) uses "sepulchre" frequently in his *Childe Harold's Pilgrimage*, in which the young Harold is traveling across Europe, bemoaning the fall of the Classical civilizations. In Athens, for example, he cries:

Look on this spot—a nation's sepulchre!
Abode of gods, whose shrines no longer burn ...

The Bible is also fond of the word; it occurs more than once in reference to Christ's tomb, and when Christ himself is railing against the hypocritical scribes and Pharisees he says they are:

... like unto whited sepulchres, which indeed appear beautiful outward, but are within full of dead men's bones and all uncleanness.

Sepulchral can mean literally "to do with a tomb or burial," as in these beautifully sepulchral lines by the seventeenth-century cleric Thomas Ken:

Sepulchral Cypress, Lawrel, Pine, and Bays, Yew, and all Trees, whose Verdure ne're decays, Are planted in long Rows, where Mourners walk.

Alternatively, it can move away from the physical tomb and be suggestive of melancholy or gloom. The American politician Everett Dirksen (1896–1969) was known for his deep bass voice and florid oratorical style; the essayist Lance Morrow (1939–2024) observed that Dirksen's delivery could be "remotely approximated by sipping twelve-year-old bourbon, straight, while reading Dickens aloud, in a sort of sepulchral purr."

Shaman

In the religions of many, and particularly the nomadic cultures of the Arctic regions of both Asia and America, a shaman is a multipurpose figure, a combination of priest, fortune-teller, healer, and intercessor between the physical and spiritual worlds. Shamans are able to SHAPE-SHIFT (see opposite), often taking on the form of a bear; they go into trances and states of ecstasy, frequently accompanied by dancing and drumming; and they converse not only with the spirits of the dead but also with birds, animals, and trees, to impart wisdom to the lay members of their communities.

The word has complicated origins that include Russian and German terms for SORCERY (see page 215) or WITCHCRAFT (see page 256), but can also be traced back, via the Tungus dialect of Siberia, to a word for "religious exercise" in Sanskrit, the ancient language of India.

Shape-shifter

Someone or something that is able to change its shape or form at will, normally through supernatural powers. For hundreds of years WEREWOLVES (see page 253), VAMPIRES (see page 243), and many other creatures from mythologies all over the world have been able to shape-shift, but the Scottish collector of folk tales Andrew Lang was one of the first to use the term, in 1887. Having observed that people imagine gods and other supernatural beings to be like themselves, he wrote:

> *Now they believe themselves to be conscious of magical and supernatural powers, which they do not, of course, possess. These powers of effecting metamorphosis, of 'shape-shifting,' of flying, of becoming invisible at will, of conversing with the dead, of miraculously healing the sick, [people] pass on to their gods.*

And, when it is appropriate, they pass them on to their werewolves and vampires too.

Shellycoat

While almost every culture has its own form of BOGEY-MAN (see page 31), each tends to have its own identifying features. This Scots variation on the theme is singled out by the coat of shells which gives him his name. According to Jacob Grimm (one of the famous fairytale-telling brothers), in his multi-volumed survey of Teutonic mythology published in 1835, the shellycoat falls into the category of "home sprites," who are benevolent, loyal to their masters, and "contented with a trifling wage: a new hat, a red cap, a parti-coloured coat with tinkling bells he will make shift with."

A German equivalent is known as *Schellenrock* or "bell coat," because his tunic is adorned not with shells but with bells. Home sprites generally laugh a lot, and making a noise when they move clearly keeps them amused.

Sheol

The New Revised Standard Version of the Old Testament, published in 1989, contains numerous references to Sheol, from the joyous "O Lord, you brought up my soul from Sheol, restored me to life from among those gone down to the Pit" to the vengeful "Let death come upon them; let them go down alive to Sheol, for evil is in their homes and in their hearts," both in the Book of Psalms. The King James Version of 1611 renders the first of these Sheols as "the grave" and the second as "hell," because Sheol can be both these things and more. It is a Hebrew word and represents the home of the dead in Hebrew culture, a place shrouded in darkness from which no one can return. In early scriptures, all the dead went there; later there developed the concept of Gan Eden (derived from the Garden of Eden) and GEHENNA (see page 82), the equivalents of the Christian Heaven and Hell, so that Sheol became the place of waiting, hanging around until God decided what a soul's fate was to be.

Sigil

Derived from the Latin for "a little sign," a sigil is just that—a seal or mark, but with magical significance. It could protect the owner, as in the case of an amulet, or in some OCCULT circles (see page 176) be used by a MEDIUM (see page 153) in a trance to enter a previous life or a state of ecstasy. Alexander Pope's 1715 poem *The Temple of Fame*, which describes a vision seen in a dream, invokes—alongside mentions of Zoroaster, Confucius, and many other philosophers—Brahmans who:

> *Made visionary fabrics round them rise,*
> *And airy spectres skim before their eyes;*
> *Of Talismans and Sigils knew the pow'r,*
> *And careful watch'd the Planetary hour.*

Silky

An 1879 work called *Notes on the folk-lore of the northern countries of England and the borders* by the poet William Henderson records that the Northumbrian village of Black Heddon had been disturbed, some eighty or ninety years previously, by the appearance of "a supernatural being, popularly called Silky, from the nature of her robes":

> *She was remarkable for the suddenness with which she would appear to benighted travellers, breaking forth upon them, in dazzling splendour, in the darkest and most lonely parts of the road.*

Having ridden with them for a short while, she would then disappear equally suddenly. Silky also had the perverse habit of cleaning an untidy house overnight, but, should she find herself in a tidy one, would "disarrange everything." Then, one day, she suddenly disappeared, leaving behind "a large rough skin filled with gold." The suggestion was that she had been the troubled ghost of someone who had died before she could reveal the hiding place of her treasure to those she had left behind.

Sinister

This was originally nothing more frightening than the Latin word for "left," but in Ancient Roman divination the left-hand side was considered unlucky. Throughout the centuries there have been widespread prejudices against being left-handed or "coming out of left field." A bend sinister in a heraldic coat of arms is a diagonal line running across the shield from bottom left to top right, indicating illegitimacy—important if there is a large inheritance to be considered. In day-to-day speech, sinister means threatening or potentially harmful, particularly in a mysterious way—when someone looks sinister, you never quite know what they are going to do next. Dickens's description of the cruel schoolteacher in *Nicholas Nickleby* gives exactly that impression:

> *Mr. Squeers's appearance was not prepossessing. He had but one eye, and the popular prejudice runs in favour of two ... The blank side of his face was much wrinkled and puckered up, which gave him a very sinister appearance, especially when he smiled, at which times his expression bordered closely on the villainous.*

For another Dickensian character with an alarming smile, see GROTESQUE (page 97).

Sisyphean

In Greek myth, Sisyphus was a mortal who had offended the gods and was punished in Hades (Hell) by being condemned to push a boulder up a hill; when it reached the top it fell back down to the bottom, so that he had to begin again, and again, for all eternity. Sisyphus gives his name to a Sisyphean task, one that will never end and that was probably completely futile in the first place. The nineteenth-century poet James Russell Lovell, based in Massachusetts, where winter snow was plentiful, used the word with reference to the hours that could be wasted by building a snowman in the garden:

> *First comes the Sisyphean toil of rolling the clammy balls till they refuse to budge farther. Then, if you would play the statuary, they are piled one upon the other to the proper height; or if your aim be masonry, whether of house or fort, they must be squared and beaten solid with the shovel.*

Skin walker

The Navajo name for this malevolent being is "in this way it goes on all fours": in the lore of this Indigenous American people a skin walker disguises itself as a wolf, coyote, or other animal by wearing its skin and walking on all fours; or it takes possession of the body of an animal or human. The Navajo recognize "medicine people" as spiritual healers who aim only to do good; skin walkers are the opposite, being opposed to traditional Navajo values.

See also WENDIGO (page 251).

Skulduggery

Sadly, there is no reason to connect this word with skulls or with digging (for buried treasure or anything else); the dictionaries say it is "of obscure origin." It means underhand behavior or intrigue, but not necessarily of a demonic kind.

In Sir Walter Scott's 1818 novel *The Heart of Mid-Lothian,* the powers that be in Edinburgh aren't convinced that honest men are what they need in order to enforce the law; such men are "feared [frightened] for this, and they are scrupulous about that, and they arena free to tell a lie, though it may be for the benefit of the city." All they'll ever discover is "a wee bit skulduddery"—some token misdemeanors. It would be much better, the authorities conclude, to employ rogues, who will have no compunction about doing what the job needs them to do.

Skull and crossbones

It may seem odd to think there could have been a Golden Age of Piracy, but there was—from about 1650 to 1730. It was the privateers of the latter part of this period who adopted an existing "death's head" flag as their symbol. Usually a white image on a black background, the skull is generally grinning; two bones crossed in the form of an X sit either beneath or behind it. From an early stage in its piratical career, the flag has also been known as the Jolly Roger, possibly because of its smiling "face" and because "Old Roger" (like "Old Nick" and "Old Harry," see POKER, page 185) is an old-fashioned, jokey name for the Devil.

The symbolism of the skull and crossbones persisted in literature through the nineteenth and early twentieth centuries. In Robert Louis Stevenson's *Treasure Island* (1883), one of the dastardly Long John Silver's first acts when he mutinies to take over the treasure-hunting ship *Hispaniola* is to replace its "British colors" with the Jolly Roger, which he calls "the black flag of piracy." In 1904 J.M. Barrie went so far as to call the pirate ship in *Peter Pan* the *Jolly Roger*. His stage directions to the original play describe the ship as "flying the skull and crossbones," but the name of the ship would have told his audience everything they needed to know about its crew, even before they met the villainous Captain Hook.

Hollywood has also always loved the Jolly Roger, to the extent that it appeared in the first filmed version of *Treasure Island* in 1912 and was still with us, with two crossed cutlasses rather than crossed bones, in the twenty-first-century series *Pirates of the Caribbean*. You sometimes see the skull wearing an eye patch or even the red headscarf that is another Hollywood-pirate favorite. But although the entertainment industry has turned it into something rather glamorous and swashbuckling, the skull and crossbones has its origins in pillaging, murder, and treachery.

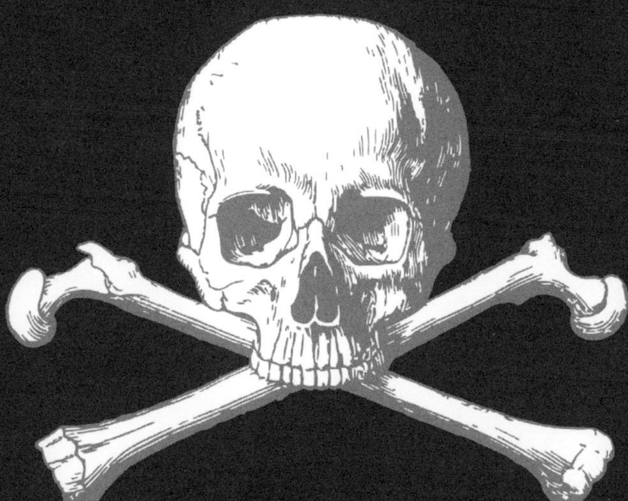

Soothsayer

Sooth is an archaic word for "truth," so a soothsayer is one who tells the truth, specifically the truth about the future: a seer or a prophet. The word has been in English since the fourteenth century, originally meaning simply someone who tells the truth. Within a hundred years, however, it had acquired the pejorative sense of someone who gains their insights through being in league with the Devil. An influential devotional text called (in modern spelling) *The Chastising of God's Children,* written around 1390, warns that:

> *Some show prophecy in the spirit of [the] Devil as are those men & women whom men call diviners, or soothsayers.*

A 1535 translation of the Bible warns, in the Book of Isaiah, that if anyone suggests that you seek counsel of "the soythsayers, witches, charmers and coniurers," you would be better advised to consult God. The same passage in the King James Bible of 1611 warns against "them that have familiar spirits, and unto wizards that peep, and that mutter," while the twentieth-century New International Version has "mediums and spiritists, who whisper and mutter." Whichever version you prefer, it's clear that soothsaying has implications far beyond simply telling the truth.

Sorcery

The *Collins English Dictionary* definition of this word is a particularly macabre one: "the art, practices, or spells of magic; esp. black magic, by which it is sought to harness occult forces or evil spirits in order to produce preternatural effects in the world." The *Chambers Dictionary* mentions magic, enchantment, and WITCHCRAFT (see page 256), but also contributes the more specific "divination by the assistance of evil spirits." This last definition comes closest to the etymological meaning of the word, which derives from the Latin for lot, in the sense of drawing lots.

The line between sorcery and witchcraft is often blurred, but the (slightly pernickety) distinction is that a witch draws on his or her innate powers, whereas a sorcerer has to learn skills and/or involve something external, such as a spirit. Most modern witches would also maintain that they use their powers for good, whereas sorcery leans firmly towards the darker and more malevolent side.

Specter

From the Latin for "to look at," this is a ghost or apparition, something that seems to appear out of nowhere. In Washington Irving's story "The Legend of Sleepy Hollow" (1820), the hero Ichabod Crane spends a cozy evening exchanging stories of GHOSTS (see page 84) and WITCHCRAFT (see page 256) with his neighbors:

> *But if there was a pleasure in all this, while snugly cuddling in the chimney corner of a chamber that was all of a ruddy glow from the crackling wood fire, and where, of course, no spectre dared to show its face, it was dearly purchased by the terrors of his subsequent walk homewards. What fearful shapes and shadows beset his path, amidst the dim and ghastly glare of a snowy night! ... How often was he appalled by some shrub covered with snow, which, like a sheeted spectre, beset his very path!*

The idiom "a specter at the feast," meaning someone or something casting a gloom over an otherwise pleasant occasion, is said to be a reference to the ghost of the murdered Banquo appearing at Macbeth's banquet in Shakespeare's play (1606). A specter can also be something unpleasant looming in the future: Karl Marx and Friedrich Engels opened *The Communist Manifesto* (1848) with a reference to "the specter of Communism" haunting Europe, before spending the rest of their famous pamphlet debunking the very suggestion that Communism was casting any sort of gloom.

Spiritualism

Originally simply a belief in the importance of things spiritual, as opposed to material, spiritualism developed in the mid-nineteenth century into the belief that the spirits of the dead could communicate with the living, usually via a MEDIUM (see page 153) and during a SÉANCE (see page 202), though it can also be a more umbrella term, bringing in PSYCHIC (see page 188) powers, TELEKINESIS (see page 228), and the use of the Ouija board (see OUIJA, page 179).

This is a belief that has always provoked extreme reactions one way or another. Sir Arthur Conan Doyle who—as we saw under ECTOPLASM (see page 63)—was a keen believer in spiritualism, wrote a letter to *The Times*, published on January 3, 1920, in which he objected to their report that he believed mediums could "raise a spirit." This turn of phrase, he asserted:

> *... would seem to imply that we had some control over those who have passed into the beyond. Such is not the case. The most that we can do is to make the physical conditions such that if they should of their own desire wish to manifest themselves to our senses, they may be able to do so.*

While he wasn't convinced of the spirits' ability to predict the future, he did believe that "From their higher ground the spirit people see the relations between cause and effect more clearly than we do." And in the same letter he went on to "solemnly declare" that:

> *... using an unpaid medium, I have beyond all question or doubt spoken face to face with my son, my brother, my nephew by marriage and several other friends since their death. On each occasion there were six or more witnesses.*

On the other hand, the American television presenter Dick Cavett (born 1936) shrugged off the entire phenomenon:

> *I have never been converted to or even had much interest in spiritualism, occultism, Swedenborgianism or any particular religion. And I never, except occasionally for a laugh, visit the quacks who call themselves psychics.*

Striga

VAMPIRE-like creatures (see page 243) from Romanian mythology, striga (the word serves as both singular and plural) are former humans now ensnared by dark magic and forced to live on the blood of other humans. Striga take various forms: some are women who have been transformed into wolves and who sneak into nurseries at night to drink the blood of babies; others are sorcerers who retain some sort of empathy for fellow humans and are more likely to prey on livestock than on people, meaning that farmers need to appease them with gifts of wheat and milk. Then there is the so-called Dead Striga, said to be the inspiration for Bram Stoker's Dracula. It rises from the grave of the recently dead and returns to that person's home in their guise, as if the death hadn't occurred. The striga then feeds on other members of the deceased's family, causing them to weaken or die, and allowing the body that the striga has taken over to continue in this world. Ramming a silver stake through the deceased's heart and/or placing a clove of garlic under their tongue was said to prevent the striga gaining access to the corpse—and gave rise to similar ploys pervading myriad Hollywood movies.

Since the world of fantasy fiction adopted the striga (notably in the *Witcher* series of books by Andrzej Sapkowski and the associated video games and Netflix series), it has endowed her with other attributes: red hair, a huge bear-like jaw, claws strong enough to tear a person apart, and a tendency to leave her grave and hunt more frequently at the time of a full moon.

Striga is said to come from the Latin *strix*, meaning owl, a bird that is often considered an omen of death; but it's also been associated with the Romanian word for to scream. And although the word "witcher" existed before Sapkowski started writing his books in the 1980s, it was initially a synonym for "witch." In Sapkowski's world, however, it is a witch hunter with magic powers who, according to the blurb for the first book in the series, "hunts the vile fiends that ravage the land and attack the innocent."

See LILITH (page 138) for another creature associated with owls and howling.

Stygian

In Greek myth, in order to enter the Underworld, you had to cross the River Styx, in a boat rowed by the ferryman Charon. He's the reason that, in some rituals, coins were placed in or near the mouth of the deceased: you had to pay the ferryman. Stygian is the adjective derived from the name of the river and normally means particularly dark, gloomy, or hellish. In Thomas Hardy's novel *The Hand of Ethelberta* (1876), an alarming noise provokes the question, "But what Stygian sound was this? There had arisen at the moment upon the mute and sleepy air a varied howling from a hundred tongues." It transpires that this particular sound isn't hellish: the characters who hear it are close to a kennel where the dogs have a frightening tendency to bark at odd hours of the night.

On a more banal level, you could leave someone in Stygian gloom simply by turning the lights out and making sure the curtains were tightly closed, but the feeling in the room would be eerie rather than cozy.

Succubus

See INCUBUS (page 120).

Taniwha

A Maori word and a Maori monster, often one in the form of a dragon or serpent that lives in the depths of the ocean or in the recesses of a cave. Some taniwhas are able to change their shape and disguise themselves as sharks, whales, or floating logs. They may be benevolent guardians—the legendary explorer Kupe, traditionally regarded as the first person to discover New Zealand, had one that guarded canoes traveling across Cook Strait, between the country's North and South Islands. But taniwhas can also be fierce, destructive creatures, known to attack and eat men or to capture women in order to make them their wives. Heroic and cunning taniwha slayers play an important role in Maori mythology, luring the monsters out of their sanctuaries in order to club or trap them, or casting spells that send them to sleep.

Taphephobia

A phobia is by definition abnormal—not a rational, "I'd rather not be in a confined space with something fluttery" sort of fear, but an over-reacting, debilitating terror. There are many words to describe specific horrors, among the most common being claustrophobia and agoraphobia, a fear respectively of confined and open spaces. Then there's ailurophobia, fear of cats; ophiophobia, fear of snakes; triskaidekaphobia, fear of the number thirteen. Fair enough, you might think—lots of people are frightened of these things. Others are more far-fetched—arctophobia, fear of teddy bears; arachibutyrophobia, fear of peanut butter sticking to the roof of your mouth; and the obviously "made up for the fun of it" hippopotomonstrosesquippedaliophobia, fear of long words.

But there is one phobia that has affected numerous historical figures, from the American president George Washington to the composer Frederic Chopin, and inspired several of the horror stories of American writer Edgar Allan Poe. Taphephobia, the first part of the word deriving from the Greek for grave, is an abnormal fear of being buried alive. Poe doesn't use the word, but the narrator of his 1844 story "The Premature Burial" is so obsessed with the idea that he has the family vault remodeled so that it can be opened from the inside and he makes arrangements for "the free admission of air and light, and convenient receptacles for food and water." His coffin, too, can be opened from the inside and within reach is a rope that will ring a bell suspended from the roof of the tomb.

> *But, alas, what avails the vigilance against the Destiny of man? Not even these well-contrived securities sufficed to save from the uttermost agonies of living inhumation, a wretch to these agonies foredoomed!*

As you might expect from Poe, this is taphephobia in a most extreme form. And it doesn't end well.

Tarasca

A dragon-like monster seen in parades marking the Christian festival of Corpus Christi, sometimes ridden by a woman who symbolizes vice. Tarasca is an Occitan or Provençal word, with a French equivalent *tarasque*, and the creature has featured in French mythology since at least the fourteenth century. "Dragon" is a loose description: among other fearsome attributes it is said to have a lion's head, six feet with bear-like claws, a body protected by a carapace like a tortoise's, and a serpent's tail. According to the tradition of the southern French city of Tarascon, it swallowed human victims head first; it also had a poisonous breath that emerged from both its mouth and its nostrils.

Tarascon sits on the river Rhone and it was here that the tarasca was said to lurk, attacking people and boats who tried to cross. It has been likened to the biblical LEVIATHAN (see page 136), but there are also obvious resemblances to La Gargouille's activities in the Seine at Rouen (see GARGOYLE, page 81).

Tarot

A pack of cards used in fortune-telling, invented in Italy in the 1430s and now consisting of 22 cards known as the Major Arcana (see ARCANE, page 14), plus four "minor" suits of 14 cards each. In a tarot reading, the Major Arcana deals with spiritual matters and important life events, while the Minor Arcana focuses on more day-to-day happenings, with each of the suits—Cups, Wands, Swords, and PENTACLES (see page 181)—dealing with different aspects of a person's life. The etymology of the word can be traced from English back through French and into Italian, but thereafter its source disappears, appropriately, into the great unknown.

Tartarus

The great judgment hall of Greek mythology, where the harsh judge Rhadamanthus hears confessions and passes sentence on the recently dead. According to the Roman poet Virgil:

he forces
Acknowledgment of crime; no man in the world,
No matter how cleverly he hides his evil,
No matter how much he smiles at his own slyness,
Can fend atonement off.

Tisiphone, the avenging Fury (see FURIES, page 79), keeps guard over the entrance; within the hall lives the fifty-headed Hydra:

her fifty throats
Are black, and open wide, and Tartarus
Is black, and open wide, and it goes down
To darkness, sheer deep down ...

So Tartarus is a place of everlasting torment and punishment for those who deserve it.

The word can also be used of other such unforgiving places. Victor Hugo, in *The Hunchback of Notre-Dame* (1831), shows the gypsy Esmeralda, under arrest for alleged WITCHCRAFT (see page 256) and attempted murder, being escorted into a gloomy, windowless chamber lined with instruments of torture: "a confused mass of horrible things." Hugo says baldly: "This Tartarus was called simply, The Question Chamber." Clearly, like the original Tartarus, it was very much more than that.

Tattie-bogle

According to dictionaries of the Scottish tongue, this is a scarecrow, particularly one set up in a potato field (and often with a potato for a head), *tattie* being the Scots word for "potato" and *bogle* a frightening PHANTOM (see page 184) or GHOST (see page 84); it can also (like "scarecrow" in standard English) be a ragged or unkempt person. In addition, it is a turnip-lantern used at HALLOWE'EN (see page 102)—a JACK O' LANTERN (see page 125), but made from a turnip rather than a pumpkin.

Although firmly entrenched in Scotland, it's likely that the idea of the turnip-lantern came from an Irish legend of a man called Stingy Jack, said to have tricked the Devil in order to make money. When Jack died, God didn't want him in Heaven and the Devil didn't want him in Hell, so he was destined to roam the Earth for ever more. Irish peasants began carving scary faces into turnips in order to frighten off Jack's unpleasant spirit.

It's highly likely that the Irish who moved to North America in large numbers after the devastating potato famines of the 1840s and '50s took this tradition with them, and began doing their carving with the pumpkin that was native to their new home.

Telekinesis

Depending on your age, you may know of this phenomenon from Stephen King's *Carrie* (1974) or Roald Dahl's *Matilda* (1988) and their various spinoffs and adaptations, but both these characters had the same gift: the ability to move objects without touching them, through sheer force of will or "magic" power. While Carrie sets fire to her school and kills a number of her classmates in the course of a disastrous prom night, Matilda uses her abilities to right injustices, but whatever its cause and its outcome, the concept of telekinesis is the same: it comes from Greek words meaning "distant" (which also gave us "television" and "telephone") and "movement" (which also gave us "cinema").

Psychokinesis is a similar, though slightly more recent, concept: telekinesis is first recorded in 1890, psychokinesis in 1914, coined by the American author and publisher Henry Holt in a book called *On the Cosmic Relation.* In this he writes extensively on the classification of these differing phenomena:

> *Now assuming Telekinesis to be established, perhaps we are as nearly ready to consider what I shall call Psychokinesis; as people were a generation ago to consider Telekinesis.*

Holt was a great coiner of terms: in the same work we also find autokinesis, "the alleged levitation of the human body by a force which apparently is generated in the body itself"; and telepsychosis, in which a MEDIUM (see page 153) receives impressions "apparently from other intelligences than his own ... derived from the minds of persons present, persons distant, and ostensibly persons no longer in the body."

In explanation of these terms, he observes ruefully, but not without a glimmer of truth:

> *... we must have a Greek name to command any respect ... But I sometimes wish we could string out names from our own roots, as do the good Germans, even if we seemed to model them as they appear to, on their dachshunds.*

Telepathy

The *tele-* part of this word, as in TELEKINESIS (see opposite), means distant; *-pathy* comes from the Greek for feeling or perception. Thus telepathy—also known as thought transference—is sharing feelings or understanding not necessarily from a great distance, but in unconventional ways, without the involvement of any tangible means of communication such as speech, writing, or sign language.

The concept first attracted wide public notice in the late nineteenth century, when not only did members of the newly founded Society for Psychical Research (SPR) attempt to analyze and "prove" it, but the American magician and stage "mentalist" Washington Irving Bishop (1855–89) began giving "thought-reading" demonstrations all over the world. He ascribed his success to "muscle sensitivity," a particularly well-honed ability to interpret his subjects' body language, though he later and controversially claimed to have supernatural powers. The term "telepathy" was coined in 1882 by Frederic Myers, one of the founders of the SPR, who wrote in the first issue of the society's journal:

> *We venture to introduce the words Telæsthesia and Telepathy to cover all cases of impression received at a distance without the normal operation of the recognised sense organs.*

Interest in telepathy didn't die with the Victorians. As recently as 2015, Mark Zuckerberg, founder of Meta, wrote in his Townhall Q & A:

> *One day, I believe we'll be able to send full rich thoughts to each other directly using technology. You'll just be able to think of something and your friends will immediately be able to experience it too if you'd like.*

Termagant

Originally a violent and arrogant (male) deity in medieval morality plays, its name deriving from an Old French term for a non-Christian god. By Shakespeare's time termagant was not necessarily a proper name, but could be used to describe any violent, quarrelsome person. They still tended to be male, though: Shakespeare doesn't use the word in *The Taming of the Shrew* (c. 1590), where the ill-tempered person of the title is a woman, but in *Henry IV, Part I* (c. 1597) he has Falstaff describe the hot-headed rebel Hotspur as "that hot termagant Scot." Less than a hundred years later, however, the essayist Richard Steele was referring to "Termagant Wives who make Wedlock a Yoke," and termagant has been applied more to women than to men ever since.

Tokoloshe

A diminutive South African water spirit that can render itself invisible by drinking water. It can then do the bidding of its evil masters undetected and cause all sorts of mayhem. In cultures where people traditionally slept on mats on the floor, raising the mat became a traditional way of protecting from tokoloshe attacks during the night, as the spirit was unable to reach anything above about hip height. (On a more mundane level, it also made it less likely that the sleepers would be suffocated by the carbon monoxide fumes from a dying fire, which, being heavier than air, sank toward ground level.) And even if you aren't sleeping on the floor near a dying fire, putting bricks under the legs of the bed remains a let's-be-on-the-safe-side way of keeping the tokoloshe at bay.

Tonton Macoute

In Haitian mythology, the equivalent of the BOGEY-MAN (see page 31), whose name translates as "Uncle Sack." Like KRAMPUS (see page 133), he would carry naughty children off in a bag but would then go a step further than Krampus by eating said children for breakfast.

The name gained more widespread recognition in the 1950s and '60s when the Haitian dictator "Papa Doc" Duvalier created a secret police force, answerable only to himself, that became notorious for its corruption, its brutal behavior, and the number of people who disappeared under its regime. Although over the years this force had other official titles, it was natural to the Haitian people to name it after something they had been brought up to fear. The Tontons Macoute are a menacing presence in Graham Greene's 1966 novel *The Comedians*, set in Haiti:

> *Luckily no one dared move on the roads at night; it was the hour when only zombies worked or else the Tontons Macoute. As for the Tontons they were certainly abroad; we heard the approach of their car—no other car would be out so late—before we reached the end of the drive.*

Further underlining his Bogey-man theme, Greene adopts another name from Haitian folklore as a nickname for Papa Doc:

> ... *we dignified his shambling shabby figure with the title of Baron Samedi [Baron Saturday], who in the Voodoo mythology haunts the cemeteries in his top-hat and tails, smoking his big cigar.*

See also LWA (page 143).

Toska

There's plenty to be sorrowful about on the Dark Side and there are many words in many languages that describe the subtleties of sorrow. The Scottish word *misslieness* is the particular kind of loneliness that comes from missing someone or something one loves; the Gaelic *cianalas* means homesickness, a longing for a place; Old English had *wintercearig*, a feeling of despondency caused by winter. One of the saddest is the Czech *litost*; widely regarded as untranslatable, it encompasses agony, humiliation, and emotional torment, helped by the fact that, as Czech-born writer Milan Kundera (1929–2023) put it, its long, stressed first syllable "sounds like the wail of an abandoned dog."

Another contender for saddest of all (and equally untranslatable) is the Russian *toska*, a spiritual anguish with no specific cause, or an unexplained longing, described by novelist Vladimir Nabokov (1899–1977) as "a dull ache of the soul."

Many translators, struggling to convey in English all that *toska* implies, opt for "melancholy," but there is much more to it than that.

Troll

A familiar term today because of the people who write aggressive and anonymous messages online, this word pre-dates the invention of social media by at least four centuries. In fact, the modern trolls take their name not from the creature that lurks beneath bridges in fairy tales but from a form of fishing—the link apparently being that an online troll is hoping to provoke (i.e. is fishing for) a response. That said, the connection with the unpleasant creature of folklore is not inappropriate.

Trolls were written about in the thirteen-century Icelandic *Eddas*, but they featured in the oral traditions of Norway, Sweden, Denmark, and Iceland before that. The Norwegian folktale *Per Gynt* (the basis of Henrik Ibsen's 1867 play *Peer Gynt* and the associated music by Edward Grieg) features a troll known as the Bøyg, who takes the form of an enormous and slimy serpent. In other early tales, a troll was a giant; later it became a dwarf, living in a cave or underground. It might have one head or two or three; it frequently had only one eye. (The appealing idea that trolls are born with one head but grow others as they age in order to frighten away other trolls seems to have come from the 2010 Norwegian movie *Trollhunter* rather than from any ancient folkloric source.)

According to an 1867 encyclopedia rejoicing in the name of *A dictionary of science, literature, & art: comprising the definitions and derivations of the scientific terms in general use, together with the history and descriptions of the scientific principles of nearly every branch of human knowledge,* trolls are engaged in a perpetual struggle against humans. They are superior in strength and stature, but far inferior in intellect, so are constantly outwitted. The Visit Norway website confirms that trolls are traditionally both dangerous and stupid, but still clever enough to ask difficult riddles before permitting you to pass should you encounter one. Once upon a time, they roamed freely in mountains and forests, but only during the hours of darkness: if they didn't retreat in time, the rising sun would turn them to stone—which is why there are so many troll-like formations in rock faces and stones all over Norway.

Tsuchigumo

See Jorogumo (page 127).

Tsujigiri

A Japanese word meaning "crossroads killing," this denotes a gruesome ritual practiced by the Samurai, the Japanese warrior class who effectively ruled the country from 1185 to 1869. The Samurai were great swordsmen and, to hone their skills and ensure that their swords were in good order, they would go out at night and attack the first person they met.

Crossroads have a long association with misfortune and death in other cultures, too: see Hecate (page 104).

Uabhas

Pronounced approximately *oo-ath-vas*, this is a Scots or Irish Gaelic word that can be translated as atrocity, consternation, dread, enormity, fright, monster, or a large quantity, a fearful amount. Etymologically, it's a combination of the words for horror and death; on a practical level, it's a useful, wide-ranging term for whenever things look grim.

Ufology

This is the study of UFOs or Unidentified Flying Objects—defined by *Encyclopedia Britannica* as "any aerial object or optical phenomenon not readily identifiable to the observer." Thought by many to be craft bringing intelligent life from other parts of the cosmos to investigate Earth, UFOs became a particular area of interest after the Second World War with the development of manned spacecraft and artificial satellites. Initially popularly called "flying saucers"—a term whose first recorded use was in *The Times* in 1947—they were officially designated "unidentified flying objects" in 1956. This was after the United States government launched Project Blue Book, a formal study of these phenomena; its brief was to discover if UFOs were a threat to national security and to analyze data of reported sightings. The term is said to have been coined by Edward J. Ruppelt, a US Air Force officer involved in the project, the explanation being that not all UFOs were saucer-shaped. Ufology, though not formally credited to Ruppelt, was coined about the same time, to describe the work that Project Blue Book was undertaking.

The project came to an end in 1969, when the powers that be decided that continued funding couldn't be justified in terms of either national security or the interests of science. A summary of Blue Book's ultimate findings attributed UFO sightings to four principal causes:

- A mild form of mass hysteria.
- Individuals who fabricate such reports to perpetrate a hoax or seek publicity.
- Psychopathological persons [those suffering from some form of mental illness].
- Misidentification of various conventional objects.

Of course, not everyone has written the entire subject off…

Uncanny

Characterized by something that cannot be easily explained, supernatural and often horrific. Originally found in Scotland and northern England, the word derives from "can" in the sense of being able to do something. Someone who is canny is shrewd, likely to be good at business, and also wary, so not easily deceived. Early meanings of uncanny were the opposite: careless, rash, unreliable, not good to do business with; later—because of all these negative qualities—something uncanny became likely to be connected with the supernatural. This was a familiar sense, in Scotland at least, by the time the poet Robert Fergusson wrote, in 1773:

For this some ca'd him an uncanny wight;
The clash gaed round, 'he had the second sight.'

In this context, "wight" simply means a being and "the clash gaed round" could be rendered "rumour had it."

In 1949 the publishers of Algernon Blackwood (1869–1951), one of the most prolific ghost-story writers of his or any other era, issued a collection called *Tales of the Uncanny and Supernatural.* It included titles such as "The Occupant of the Room," "The Terror of the Twins," and "The Empty Sleeve"—a reasonable cross-section of what the word *uncanny* could possibly encompass.

Ushabti

The ancient Egyptians were very keen on "grave goods": items buried with the dead to help them live comfortably in the next world. These could include food and drink, plates and goblets, chariots, servants—and *ushabti*. Also called *shabti*, these were figurines, often produced en masse and not much more than six inches high, made from anything from wax to stone or ceramic, depending on the period and on the wealth of the deceased. *Ushabti* generally carried hoes over their shoulders and baskets on their back, ready for any farm work that needed to be done, but hieroglyphic inscriptions on some figures suggest that they were prepared to do whatever the gods asked them to do. It's not clear where the word comes from, but it may be connected with the ancient Egyptian for "follower" or "answerer," because of the *ushabtis'* willingness to do as they were told.

Vampire

A malevolent being, often one that comes out of the grave at night, who feeds on the blood of someone sleeping. There have been legends of blood-sucking creatures throughout the world for many centuries, but the vampire as we know it (and specifically as incarnated by Bram Stoker's *Dracula*—see NECROMANCY, page 167) developed in the lore of Transylvania, a province of modern Romania, in the Middle Ages. The word came into English from French in the eighteenth century (well over a century before Bram Stoker made it his own), but exists in similar forms in languages all over Europe, from Hungarian to Portuguese.

That first eighteenth-century occurrence appears in the anonymous 1734 work *Travels of Three English Gentlemen, from Venice to Hamburgh.* The gentlemen of the title, visiting an area that probably now corresponds to northern Hungary, come across stories of vampires and quote someone they describe as "a Person of great Erudition" as having written:

> *The Vampyres, which come out of the Graves in the Night-time, rush upon People sleeping in their Beds, suck out all their Blood, and destroy them. They attack Men, Women, and Children, sparing neither Age nor Sex. The People attacked by them complain of Suffocation, and a great Interception of Spirits; after which, they soon expire.*

This same erudite person also apparently wrote that the vampires' hair and nails continued to grow after death, and that their bodies showed not the least "Mark of Corruption," while others, dead for the same length of time, were "perfectly putrefied."

Vodník

This water spirit goes by various names across East Central Europe: *vodník* is the Czech one, with *vodyanoy* the Slavic equivalent. Both translate simply as "waterman." It's not a very accurate name, however, as the vodník has SHAPE-SHIFTING abilities (see page 205) and often takes the form of a frog. In his human form he may be naked and bald with a pot belly, or he may have green hair and a long, green beard. When he emerges from the water, he may be covered in algae and mud. Some versions of his story give him red eyes that shine like hot coals and webbed feet with long talons instead of hands.

Whatever his appearance, he has a short temper and is prone to breaking dams and causing flooding and drowning, dragging people down into his underwater realm to serve as his slaves.

In some traditions the *rusalka*, a female water spirit, features as the vodník's wife (though in Antonín Dvorak's 1901 opera *Rusalka* she is his daughter). She may be benevolent toward humans; or she may be the spirit of a young woman who has drowned, often in an act of suicide after an unhappy marriage or unwanted pregnancy. Less benevolent in this form, she has been known to entangle young men in her long, flowing hair and drown them in revenge for her treatment on Earth.

Spirits who drown humans in a fit of temper are not confined to Eastern Europe. The Japanese have the *kappa* or "river child," who drags not only people but horses and cattle into the water. Depicted as a vaguely human-like figure, green and slimy but with a turtle's carapace, the *kappa* has the unusual characteristics of being keen on sumo wrestling and cucumbers.

See LA LLORONA (page 141) for another figure implicated in drownings.

Voodoo

From a West African word for spirit, voodoo crossed the Atlantic to the Caribbean Islands and the Southern United States with the enslaved people of the seventeenth century, although the word is not found in English until the nineteenth century. It's a form of religious observance that once included such wide-ranging practices as serpent worship, human sacrifice, cannibalism, WITCHCRAFT (see page 256), and the use of FETISHES (see page 75) to keep oneself safe and/or bring harm to others. Most of these have fallen into abeyance, although practitioners are still able to enter a trance state in order to communicate with ancestors and animistic deities. Voodooism also has a gentler side, embracing herbal remedies that, for example, ease the pains of childbirth.

By the end of the nineteenth century, voodoo was also being used pejoratively and loosely to describe any sort of superstitious or dark magical practices: to "put a voodoo on someone" is much the same as putting a HEX on them (see page 111), intending to bring them bad luck. The widespread concept of a voodoo doll, an image of a person into which you stick pins as another way of causing them ill fortune, stems from this casual usage rather than from the religion itself.

See also LWA (page 143) and TONTON MACOUTE (page 232).

Waking

Not so much "waking up" as "keeping awake," this was a form of torture designed to make a supposed witch confess, widely used in Scotland in the sixteenth century. The suspect was fitted with an iron bridle whose prongs pushed into her mouth; she was then chained to a wall, so that she was unable to lie down. If she showed any signs of falling asleep (surely unlikely in this position), her jailers were on hand to prod her awake again. After a few days of sleep deprivation, she would begin to hallucinate and anything she said would make her sound as if she were possessed by a demon—a sure sign of guilt.

Walpurgisnacht

Since time immemorial May 1 has been dedicated to celebrating the return of spring, the growth of crops, the protection of both people and livestock, and fertility in all its forms (hence the phallic maypole still often seen on English village greens). It's not difficult to imagine that such a celebration came to feature sex, alcohol, and riotous behavior. In the Pagan world the night of April 30/May 1 is Beltane, one of the four great SABBATS of the year (see page 195), also marking the return of spring. But to medieval Christians in what is now Germany it was the night when the powers of darkness partied on the Brocken, the highest peak in the Harz mountains, and evil forces were out and about. In order to combat this, who better to invoke than a saint who had, in her lifetime, gained a reputation for battling witchcraft (as well as pests and rabies) and whose feast day also happened to be May 1?

The saint in question was Walpurga, an eighth-century Anglo-Saxon missionary who had been sent from England to Germany to convert the locals to Christianity. It's from her that the festival gets its name, *Walpurgisnacht* being German for "Walpurga's Night" or "the night before Walpurga's Day."

Today the Christian and the Pagan festivals have morphed into one in many parts of northern Europe, with the bonfires, dressing up, playing tricks on friends and family, and hanging sprigs of "sacred" foliage to ward off evil spirits that mark the occasion all being reminiscent of early Pagan traditions.

Warlock

The male equivalent of a witch, from Old English words meaning "dissembler, one who breaks an oath." Fifteen hundred years ago, that was the principal sense of "warlock"; it could also mean the Devil himself. Only later—around the year 1400 and initially in Scotland and the north of England—did it take on the modern meaning of someone in league with the Devil, possessed of evil powers. Warlocks' power must have been waning in Scotland by the time of Sir Walter Scott (1771–1832): in his novel *The Black Dwarf*, one superstitious character frets that "The wizard and the witch are the abomination and the evil thing in the land," but her son reassures her that "I am in the mind that witches and warlocks havena half the power they had lang syne"—that is, in times gone by.

You can't keep a determined demon down, though: warlocks persist in the modern fantasy world. The 1989 movie *Warlock*, about a son of Satan determined to destroy the world, spawned two sequels, and there are board games called not only Warlock but Warlock's Eye, Warlocks of the Dark Star, and many more.

Wasgo

Also known as Gonakadet, this is a sea wolf in the folklore of the Haida and Tlingit peoples of the Pacific North West of Canada and is that rare thing, a benevolent sea monster. Its goodwill continues even after death, apparently: in a story related by the artist and folklorist Bill Reid (1920–98), a poor fisherman, constantly nagged by his mother-in-law for supposed laziness, catches a Wasgo in his net. He skins it, disposes of the carcass, and wears the skin when he next goes fishing, in a lake so deep that people often drown and disappear there. On his first venture out, he catches the largest halibut he has ever seen, proceeding day by day to two halibuts, three halibuts, then moving on to orcas and finally coming home with three orcas so impressive that the nagging mother-in-law faints and dies on the spot.

Variations of the story suggest that anyone who sees Gonakadet or hears his sorrowful call will be blessed with wealth and good luck, without necessarily having to sacrifice their mother-in-law in the process.

Wendigo

A malevolent spirit in the Algonquian lore of North America, a wendigo takes possession of humans and causes them to feel insatiable and often cannibalistic hunger. The word gained notoriety beyond its Indigenous culture thanks to *The Wendigo*, a 1910 novella by Algernon Blackwood (see UNCANNY, page 240), in which two Scotsmen on a hunting trip in the Canadian wilderness are terrified by a vile and unexplained odor, massive footprints in the snow, and the appearance of a hideously deformed monster. Half a century later, Marvel Comics took hold of the idea and created not so much a monster as a curse, again haunting the snowy backwaters of Canada and sometimes translating into a YETI-like creature (see page 263) of superhuman strength, pitted against WOLVERINE (see page 261), the Hulk, and various hapless visitors to the area. A 2001 movie, *The Wendigo*, set in a wintry weekend in upstate New York, and a 2022 one with the same title, set in Northern Carolina, both continued to exploit the idea.

The word is a borrowing from several Native American languages, but its original meaning is unclear.

Werewolf

The etymology isn't definite, but "werewolf" is usually said to come from the Old English for "man wolf," and that's certainly what the word means. Being a werewolf can be proactive or reactive: either you have the power to turn into a wolf whenever you like; or you are under some spell (often activated by the full moon) that turns you into a wolf whether you like it or not. The word and the concept are found in Old English—several centuries before the Norman Conquest of 1066—though the idea seems really to have taken off in the early Middle Ages. King Cnut, who famously failed to turn back the tide and who ruled England from 1016 to 1035, wrote a book of Ecclesiastical Ordinances, one of which aimed to ensure that "the madly audacious werewolf do[es] not too widely devastate, nor bite too many of the spiritual flock." Fifty years earlier, a traveler in the Bulgarian Empire had recorded a rumor about one of the emperor's sons, said to be "such an adept in the art of magic that he could suddenly turn himself before men's eyes into a wolf or any other beast you pleased." Werewolves, like ordinary wolves (and WOLVERINES, see page 261), were said to have voracious appetites, roaming at night, stealing and eating babies, and even robbing graves in order to consume the corpses.

There were werewolf "witch trials" across Europe and as far east as Syria until the early eighteenth century, and as late as 1863 the Irish historian and folklorist Walter Keating Kelly was writing that "stories about werewolves are still current in Germany."

Then, of course, Hollywood came along: the first movie about a werewolf was a short silent of 1913 concerning a Navajo woman who turned into a timber wolf (see SKIN WALKER, page 210); in the century or so since there have been movies setting werewolves loose in London, Paris, a women's prison, and a girls' dormitory, among many, many others. The hide of traditional (pre-Hollywood) werewolves could fend off bullets and stab wounds, unless the weapon involved had been blessed in a chapel dedicated to St Hubert, patron saint of huntsmen. The idea that they can be killed by a silver bullet seems to have arisen from a misreading of an eighteenth-century French text and owes its popularity to cinema scriptwriters.

Wicca

A modern Pagan belief system, drawing on pre-Christian Celtic traditions and emphasizing the worship of nature. Formulated in the mid-twentieth century, it gained widespread recognition—and indeed legality in Britain—following the repeal of the 1735 Witchcraft Act, which (amazingly) didn't happen until 1951. Wicca marks the passing of the seasons in a cycle known as the Wheel of the Year, punctuated by the various SABBATS described in this book (see page 195). The word takes its name from the same Old English source as WITCH (see WITCHCRAFT, page 256) but, although Wiccans believe in the power of magic, the movement has no involvement with the Devil and views a witch not as a diabolic sorceress but as any initiate into its religion.

Widdershins

Also spelled withershins, this is the "wrong" direction—contrary to the way the sun appears to move, or counterclockwise. Going round something widdershins is considered by many (particularly in Scotland) to be unlucky, or to be linked to the Devil. The Scottish mathematician and demonologist George Sinclair (c.1630–96), in his *Satan's Invisible World Discovered*, described the trial of a supposed witch named Agnes Simpson, whose testimony included a witch dance in a churchyard during which "the men turned nine times Widder-shines about, and the Women six times." The ceremony that followed—conducted by the Devil in the likeness of a man—involved opening a number of graves, cutting the fingers, toes, and noses off the corpses, and passing them around the group.

It might be safer, all things considered, to go *deasil or deiseal*—clockwise, toward the right.

The word "widdershins" derives from a German term for "contrariwise," while *deasil* is Gaelic for "toward the right."

Witchcraft

The idea of a person who is to be despised, feared, and—from the sixteenth century—persecuted because they practiced or were alleged to practice magic has been with us since the English language began. A word sounding very like witch or WICCA (see page 254), derived from early Germanic languages, is found in Old English or Anglo-Saxon, making it perhaps 1,500 years old. The term "witchcraft"—the supposed use of magical powers for malevolent purposes—is about the same age.

Medieval meanings of witch overlap with those of NIGHTMARE (see page 172), referring to a spirit or monster that settled on someone while they were asleep and made them feel as if they were suffocating. But this sense was drifting away by the end of the sixteenth century, leaving us with the conventional idea of an evil old woman with a pointed hat and a flying broomstick.

No one is quite sure where the idea of the pointed witch's hat came from—anything from antisemitism to female brewers being accused of producing poor-quality beer has been suggested—but certainly it was well established by the early eighteenth century. The broomstick or besom has been associated with the OCCULT (see page 176) for even longer, though the flying part was originally attributed to the use of a "flying ointment" derived from any one of a number of magical/poisonous plants (see BELLADONNA, page 27, and MONKSHOD, page 159, for two examples). The classical scholar Richard Payne Knight (1751–1824) wrote a commentary on the *Malleus Maleficarum* in which he noted:

> *When the witch prepared to attend* [*a meeting*], *she went to her bedroom, stripped herself naked, and anointed her body with an ointment made for the purpose. She next took a staff, which also in many cases she anointed, and, placing it between her legs and uttering a charm, she was carried through the air, in an incredibly short space of time, to the place of meeting. Bodin* [*a sixteenth-century French philosopher*] *discusses learnedly the question whether the witches were really carried through the air corporeally or not; he decides it in the affirmative.*

Considering that *Malleus Maleficarum* was first published in 1486, and Bodin's *On the Demonomania of the Sorcerers* in 1580, it's safe to say that this concept too has been around for a very long time.

Brooms are also symbolic in a more positive way: in a handfasting ritual—the Wiccan ceremony of marriage—and in many other cultures, from Irish to African-American, the union is sealed by the couple involved jumping over a broomstick laid on the ground.

Witching hour

Midnight, the time when witches are most likely to appear and supernatural phenomena to occur. At one highly charged point in Shakespeare's *Hamlet* (c. 1599), Hamlet reflects on how the hour matches his mood:

> *'Tis now the very witching time of night,*
> *When churchyards yawn, and hell itself breathes out*
> *Contagion to this world. Now could I drink hot blood,*
> *And do such bitter business as the day*
> *Would quake to look on.*

Wizard

Etymologically connected with "wise," this began—in the fifteenth century or so—as a word for a wise man or philosopher, not necessarily having anything to do with magic or the "dark arts." The magical sense came along perhaps a hundred years later, with many sixteenth-century writers mentioning wizards in the same breath as witches, astrologers, and sorcerers and suggesting that they, or those who consulted them, were in league with the Devil.

Interestingly, an early-twentieth-century translation of Geoffrey of Monmouth's twelfth-century *Histories of the Kings of Britain,* from which we get much of the King Arthur legend, applies the word "wizard" to the advisers of another king, who are able to predict the sex of an unborn child. But Geoffrey's translator doesn't use it of Arthur's mentor Merlin; in fact, Merlin uses his powers to dumbfound the wizards, who are clearly charlatans. But over the centuries the word acquired more positive connotations, both in the strictly magical context and in the sense of someone who is particularly talented in their field—financial wizards, math wizards, and the like have been praised enthusiastically since the nineteenth century.

Wolfssegen

Translating (from German) as "wolf charm," this was an incantation or spell used in Bavaria to protect against wolves, particularly during the mini Ice Age of the seventeenth century, when wolves were numerous in that area. In earlier centuries, itinerant *Wolfssegner* or wolf charmers had made a living selling wolf-repelling spells or talismans until the tide turned against them in the 1590s and they began to be prosecuted as witches or even occasionally as WEREWOLVES (see page 253). More sophisticated methods of keeping wolves at bay eventually made both the charms and the charmers obsolete, though it has been suggested that the idea that werewolves can be killed by a silver bullet originated in the *Wolfssegner*'s practices.

Wolverine

In real life, this is the animal *Gulo luscus,* also known as "the glutton" because of its voracious appetite, and renowned for its fearlessness and ability to face up to creatures twice its size. Part of the weasel family, it looks like a small, solidly built, tree-climbing bear. In the darker world of Marvel comics, Wolverine is a mutant with incredibly long claws who possesses many of the characteristics of his real-life namesake, plus an uncontrollable temper and the ability to heal quickly after incurring any wounds or damage. The word "wolverine" derives from wolf, but—appropriately enough for a mutant—no one is sure how it acquired its current form.

Yeti

A word taken from the Sherpa language of the Himalayas, first used in English—in a report in *The Times*—in 1937. The Tibetan term *meetoh kangmi*, which translates as "abominable snowman," had appeared in the same newspaper in 1921. Both these instances, and subsequent ones—including the 1975 memoir of the "conqueror of Everest" Edmund Hillary—have two features in common. One, the description of the yeti as a hairy beast, something between an ape and a human, about 5ft 6in (1.7m) in height. Two, the fact that although he seems to leave a lot of footprints, no one has seen the creature himself.

The idea of a mysterious, elusive, large-footed creature living somewhere in the wilderness is not confined to the Himalayas: in the heavily forested Pacific Northwest area of Canada and the USA lurks Sasquatch, whose name comes from the Salish language and translates as "hairy man." Larger than the yeti—some (admittedly unsubstantiated) reports have Sasquatch as tall as 15ft (4.6m)—he is also commonly and prosaically called Bigfoot. In the Australian outback you may find—or at least go looking for—the Yowie, also known for his large footprints; his name is found back in 1895 in the writings of a missionary called William Ridley, who had a particular interest in the Indigenous languages. The word *Yowie* is said to derive from the name of a dream spirit who roamed the Earth at night.

Yowie

See Yeti (above).

Yuputka

A term from the Ulwa language of Nigeria, used to describe the terrifying feeling of walking in the woods at night and imagining that something—a snake? a spider? a spirit?—is crawling over your skin. English possesses two rather charming but little-used words that are relevant here: ***noctivagant***, meaning roaming by night, and ***nemophilist***, someone who loves woods and forests. Neither of these words makes the flesh creep in the way that *yuputka* does, however.

Zombie

A spirit of the dead taking over another, living body, originally in West African tradition but later more often associated with Haiti in the Caribbean. According to the (British) *Universal Magazine of Knowledge and Pleasure* in the 1780s, Zombies (spelled with a capital back then) featured large in the superstition of the Black population of Haiti: "They are supposed to be the spirits of dead wicked men, that are permitted to wander, and torment the living." That's more or less what those same spirits have done in the legions of zombie-themed movies that have appeared almost since the beginning of cinematic history. In *White Zombie* (1932), a young woman is turned into a zombie by an evil VOODOO master (see page 245), played by Bela Lugosi (fresh from his success as Dracula the previous year). In *Night of the Living Dead* (1968), the flesh-eating monsters are referred to as GHOULS (see page 85), but the principle is the same: seven people are trapped in a lonely farmhouse and the zombies will eat them if they can. In the post-apocalyptic *Friend of the World* (2020), the "zombies" are mutating creatures that may have been poisoned by radiation; and *Queens of the Dead* (2025) features Brooklyn drag queens who must use their individual talents to battle a group of zombies anxious to steal their brains. Clearly—in the movie theater at least—zombies can move with the times.

Sources and acknowledgments

The *Oxford English Dictionary* is an invaluable resource for anyone seeking information about early uses of words, while the websites www.biblegateway.com/ and www.biblestudytools.com provide multiple translations of the Bible. The episode of the BBC podcast *Uncanny*, broadcast from the Hay Festival on June 20, 2025 and available (at the time of writing) on BBC Sounds had fascinating insights into the activities of poltergeists.

The author would also like to thank the following:
page 39: From *Stiff: The Curious Lives of the Human Cadavers* by Mary Roach. Copyright © 2003 by Mary Roach. Published by Penguin. Reprinted by permission of Penguin Books Limited and used by permission of W. W. Norton & Company, Inc.; page 61: "The Problem with the Future: An Interview with Alexander Weinstein" by Garry Craig Powell, originally published in Rain Taxi Online Edition, Winter 2016; page 64: From *Net of Magic* by Lee Siegel, University of Chicago Press, 1991; page 67: Susie Dent, *Guilty By Definition* (originally published in 2024 by Zaffre, an imprint of Bonnier Books UK); page 98 from *Freeze Frame* by Peter May © Peter May, 20210, published by Quercus, reproduced by kind permission by David Higham Associates; page 140 From *The Frozen People* by Elly Griffiths, Quercus Publishing Limited, 2025. Reproduced with permission of the Licensor through PLSclear; page 198 From *The Moon and Sixpence* by W. Somerset Maugham published by Arrow. Copyright © The Royal Literary

Fund, 1919. Reprinted by permission of The Random House Group Limited; page 202 © Sarah Penner, *The London Seance Society* (Legend Press, 2023), reproduced with kind permission of Legend Press; page 233 From Graham Green, *The Comedians*, published by Random House, Vintage © Verdant Sàrl.

Ideas for possible entries for this book and information about them also came from: Ambrose Bierce, *The Devil's Dictionary* (Neale Publishing Company, 1911); Thomas Bulfinch, *The Age of Fable* (Harper & Row, 1966; Christopher Foyle, *Foyle's Philavery* (Chambers Harrap, 2007); Michael Jordan, *Witches* (Kyle Cathie, 1996); and, in no particular order:
www.babbel.com/en
www.dsl.ac.uk/
www.hrp.org.uk/tower-of-london/
www.writinginmargins.weebly.com/the-denham-tracts.html
www.gutenberg.net.au/ebooks06/0600111h.html
www.mangolanguages.com/
www.sophiasociety.org/liminal-spaces/resting-in-liminal-space
www.bbc.co.uk/programmes/articles/bfN7VPDQxynYbZbrhbjYrK/the-story-of-the-witch-farm
www.amhsnewspaper.com/19447/mythical-monsters/mythical-monsters-the-striga/
www.visitnorway.com/things-to-do/art-culture/the-mythical-norwegian-trolls/
www.bigfootencounters.com/creatures/hejkal.htm
www.romancingthegothic.com/2021/05/03/extract-on-vampires-from-the-travels-of-three-gentleman-1733-published-1745/
www.thegrandguignol.com/history
www.thecourier.co.uk/fp/news/3814009/halloween-neeps-tattie-bogle/
www.folklorethursday.com/material-culture/gargoyles-demons-sky-grotesque-guardian-angels/
www.sandyriverreview.com/2019/02/20/creepin-it-real-the-church-grim/
acred-texts.com/pag/mm/index.htm
www.gothichorrorstories.com/witches-garden/witch-garden-feature/witches-garden-plants/henbane/
www.woodlandtrust.org.uk/trees-woods-and-wildlife/fungi-and-lichens/dead-mans-fingers/
www.annwnfoundation.com/ians-blog/pwyll-pen-annwn-shapeshifting-and-the-fith-fath
yokai.com/

Index

Published in 2026 by
Rizzoli Universe, a division of
Rizzoli International Publications

Rizzoli International Publications Inc
49 West 27th Street
New York, NY 10001

Rizzoli International Publications UK Ltd
Somerset House, West Wing
Strand, London WC2R 1LA

www.rizzoliusa.com

Publisher: Charles Miers
Associate Publisher: Tina Persaud
Senior Editor: Kristy Richardson
Production Manager: Michelle Wells

A CIP catalogue record for this book is available from the British Library.

ISBN: 9780789346728

2026 / 1

MIX Paper | Supporting responsible forestry FSC® C005748

Printed in China

The authorized representative in the EU for safety and compliance is Mondadori Libri S.p.A., via Gian Battista Vico 42, Milan, Italy, 20123, www.mondadori.it

Visit us online: Instagram.com/RizzoliBooks
Facebook.com/RizzoliNewYork
Youtube.com/user/RizzoliNY

A Midnight Treasury *of* *Frightening Words*